WORLD OF SQUASH 75

Edited by Mike Palmer

Queen Anne Press London

House Editor: **Kirsty Nicholson**
Designer: **Pete Pengilley**

Photographs supplied by Tony Duffy unless otherwise credited.

Published by Queen Anne Press Limited, 12 Vandy Street, London EC2A 2EN.
Filmset in Monophoto Photina by Filmtype Services Limited, Scarborough.
Printed and bound by Hazell Watson & Viney Limited, Aylesbury, Bucks.

CONTENTS

EDITORIAL PREFACE

The idea of a squash yearbook was, initially, an instinctive reaction to the comparative dearth of general information about the game. If other sports, perhaps better established in the mind of the general public but with a smaller participant following than squash, can command regular channels of information, then squash deserved to be better served. That at least was the feeling, if not the hard economic justification for delving into the strangely introverted world of squash, a world that in the past has been embarrassed at the prospect of a bold headline.

That feeling has mellowed during the time taken to produce this book to an understanding that two years, or even one year, ago the time would not have been right. Squash has experienced rapid expansion during the last 10 years; but the appetite of players and the viewing public, encouraged by increasing media coverage, is only now beginning to demand material of a general nature to complement the existing library of instructional and coaching manuals.

Despite its strong participant nature, squash still needs its shop-window, its stars, its big events, and the aura of glamour and achievement produced by the top players.

This book is mainly about the world's better players. There is no apology for that, for they set the game's standards. It is also an attempt to reflect the world-wide growth of squash and, for the first time, to put down in biographical form the background of the players who hold the tournament scene together at the highest level.

As editor and compiler I am aware that it is not an exhaustive work. In defence, I plead that the squash world is a fragmented one, and communications within it are as yet unreliable. But the general level of cooperation has been magnificent. Without the help of correspondents and friends from all over the world, and in particular my good friend Rob Jolly, this book would not have been possible.

A pattern has been set for the future.

REVIEW OF THE SEASON

Squash will never be the same again. How can it be? The emergence of player power and a pocket-sized dynamo by the name of Qamar Zaman have wrought fundamental changes in the game.

The sight of Geoff Hunt losing his Open title, and a lean-looking Jonah Barrington, frustratingly and sadly unable to reach his former heights, showed another side of the coin. The successful staging of the world's richest professional series proved that big business can invest in squash and achieve a satisfactory return. The opening of a national centre at Wembley gave squash a home with facilities good enough to encourage television. And those who watched the European amateur team championships in Dublin saw Sweden finish third to England and Scotland. The message from Europe, and the Swedes in particular, was clear – standards are rising.

But it was Zaman, with his jet-black hair, flashing eyes, and wicked grin, who brought the season alive. The artistry of his performance against Hunt in the British Open will not be quickly forgotten by those fortunate enough to have watched it. Zaman's win was even more welcome because it was unexpected. Some of his earlier matches in Britain had been notable, but few reckoned he could survive the mental and physical pressures that Hunt would impose.

Zaman beat Hunt again in the Durham Open, and then returned home to a hero's welcome. The plane at Karachi Airport had to taxi to another section to avoid the crowds. Since then, Zaman has turned professional, along with Mohibullah Khan, to pose a constant financial threat to the more established players. Had their decision to join the paid ranks come earlier, it might have avoided the confrontation that occurred between players and governing body.

Player power is now well-established; the new professionals' association quickly got its teeth into the question of amateurs, prize-money, and levels of expenses. The professionals showed that though they were new to squash politics, as an official band their presence could not be denied. It was unfortunate that a pro tournament was cancelled because neither side would give way – but

When a title changed hands. Qamar Zaman's historic meeting with Geoff Hunt when the Australian lost his status as the world's leading player.

lessons have been learned. The pros know that they have a case, but that they must tread warily.

Jonah Barrington, despite his known dislike for establishment or authority, is emerging as a tough but respected negotiator for the pros. This may give a hint of Barrington's future in squash – which could well lie in a more entrepreneurial role. He speaks well and wins confidences . . . but can he win another Open title?

Geoff Hunt can certainly win again. The way in which he tackles Zaman in the future will be the key. Barrington believes that Hunt has not yet realised his full potential, and can become an even greater player; certainly there is no better sportsman than the Australian. He was emotionally and physically drained when Zaman beat him at Wembley, yet stood back, accepting with good grace the rush of Pakistanis on to the court who showed scant respect to the loser. Hunt admitted that Zaman 'was too good', but retained his personal dignity in a manner that won him much respect.

Unfortunately no television company was able to use this match as its screening from Wembley. The BBC's coverage of the final was generally accepted as about the best British attempt to put squash on the small screen. But more could be done; it seems to be a question of the BBC satisfying themselves that squash is television material, as well as solving the technical problems. Some people in authority at the BBC are known to view the game sceptically as entertainment, and it seems likely that we will have to be content – for the forseeable future at least – with a twice-yearly spot. This is a pity, because Wembley, purpose-built for television coverage, deserves to be used, especially as so much money has been poured into the design of one court.

The attitude of television companies tends to colour that of big commercial companies who might otherwise be tempted to put money into squash. But Yellow Dot Sportswear and British Caledonian combined in 1975 to prove that squash can justify the expense of a high prize-money circuit. The eight-man professional series (won by Hunt, the season's top cash-earner despite his title loss) gave a lift to squash – much needed after similar circuits have been vaunted and then have failed to take place.

Eventually the pros will look seriously to Europe. The game there at the moment is amateur, and while it develops is likely to remain so. But interest in watching the squash élite is bound to result in the staging of professional events. This is nothing new for Sweden; the Swedes are keen and take the game very seriously. They like to watch the best in action and judging by their performance in Dublin they learn quickly. But look out for Holland and eventually, Germany.

THE HISTORY OF SQUASH

John Horry

If the origins of squash are fairly well defined, its early history is shrouded in complete obscurity. The game has no early bibliography, nor is it mentioned in any book until nearly 50 years after it was first played.

Squash was not the brainchild of any one person as lawn tennis was, for instance. Everything is owed to its natural parent, rackets. The history of rackets is similarly vague, owing much in its turn to fives.

Rackets of a sort was played in the Fleet debtors' prison in London in the latter part of the 18th century. This was the open court variety, played in the open air. In the 19th century courts began to be built, and in 1822 Harrow became the first school to play the game.

Sometime between 1845 and 1850 a closed rackets court must have been constructed there, and it was alongside this court that squash was said to have been born. Boys waiting their turn to play rackets used a space by the side of the court to get their eye in by hitting a ball round the three-sided space. The area was too small for fast rackets balls to be used, particularly as there was no back to the 'court', so a soft rubber ball was used instead. Nothing is known about either the rackets or the balls with which the game was played, although it is obvious that the same rackets were used as in the senior game – possibly with shortened handles.

The popularity of the new game spread in the school, so that those houses that had three or even two convenient walls were used for squash. The name of the game seems to have been derived from the squashy sound made by the ball on impact compared with the firm 'plop' of the harder, faster rackets ball.

One of the celebrated Harrow names for many generations is Verney, and a member of that family refers, in a letter to his parents in 1850, to 'playing squash' at the school. As the boys at Harrow grew up and left, a number of them wanted to continue playing this easy and healthy game. It had many advantages over rackets; the main ones were that the court was so much smaller and consequently cheaper to construct, and since the game did not make the same demands on either rackets or balls, they lasted longer.

Although the original 'court' consisted of brick walls and an asphalt floor, these materials were not always used, possibly because of expense. Many of the early courts were built entirely of wood, as indeed many still are for the American version of the game. Wooden floors did not come into use until it became customary to build a roof overhead.

It is almost inconceivable that there is no history of the game prior to 1920, more than 70 years after it had first been played at Harrow. Certainly there was no competitive play in England before that date, although national championships are recorded as having taken place in the USA (1906), South Africa (1910), and Canada (1911).

What happened in these dark ages of the game, between 1850 and 1920, is largely a matter for conjecture. Owners of country houses, probably Old Harrovians, built private courts as a means of entertaining their house-party guests when the weather made outdoor sports impracticable: quite early on, roofs were added for the same reason. Even today, there are quite a number of these courts tucked away in the grounds of country houses throughout England – courts constructed of all sorts of materials, and of all sorts of sizes, for there was at that time no governing body to lay down standards.

From Harrow the game spread to other public schools, although it was not until many years had elapsed that squash was recognized as an official game, largely because it was not a 'team game' (lawn tennis had to overcome the same disadvantage). Neither was squash popular in schools that had rackets professionals, many of whom refused to let their most promising pupils play the slower game, because it was thought to harm their rackets shots. It speaks volumes for the resilience of the game that it has managed to overcome both these disadvantages.

Long before the construction of the first squash clubs, there were two other spheres in which squash started to flourish – the Army and London's West End clubs.

The Indian Army did not spend its entire life fighting in the North-West Frontier Province, and to relieve the tedium of barrack life, a number of rackets courts were built for the officers. The expense of playing the game and the difficulties of procuring the very expendable rackets and balls considerably restricted the use of those courts. So the arrival of squash was a godsend, not only to the British officers, but also to the ball boys, usually the sons of the professionals, who were all Pathans.

Some rackets courts were converted into squash courts, while a number of completely new courts were built all over what is now Pakistan. The ball boys and their descendants, of whom the most famous is Hashim Khan, have played a large part in the recent development of the game both here and in America, and today Pakistan has arguably the best players in the world.

GREAT BRITAIN 1974–75

Rex Bellamy

BRITISH OPEN

The British open championship was unusually dramatic and, in many ways, marked the end of one era and the beginning of another. Yet some of its superficially fresh features were, on second thoughts, familiar: it was played in London for the first time in seven seasons; it was won by an artist, rather than a craftsman, for the first time in nine seasons (Abou Taleb was the last champion to play as adroitly as Qamar Zaman); it was won by a Pakistani – specifically, a Pathan – for the first time in 12 seasons. So 1975 was a year in which old patterns were restored.

But in two related areas the first open championship to be played at Wembley was clearly a child of the seventies. Benson and Hedges offered a record total of £4,385 in prize-money. And generally increasing rewards from prize-money and endorsements had attracted to squash a growing band of itinerant, ambitious, and highly trained full-time players. The level of performance among them was so even that seven probably had a chance of winning. The seeding list was shattered – and in the final, the eighth seed, Zaman, beat the third seed, Gogi Alauddin.

The quarter-finals were the round that set the pulse racing, though there was much distinguished and exciting squash before that. In the first round the massive Kevin Shawcross, bulging with muscles, was taken to five games by Neven Barbour, the New Zealand champion. Equally remarkable, but for brevity rather than length, was the match in which Alauddin – understandably confident after recent wins over Geoff Hunt and Jonah Barrington – conceded only one point to a British international, John Richardson. In the second round Shawcross had another good scrap, this time with Bill Reedman, who conceded four stone but beat him. Mohibullah Khan, twice British amateur champion, handled Mike Corby with impressive authority.

With 16 players left, two of Britain's three survivors, Philip Ayton and John Easter, played some fine squash but could not stay the course with Zaman and Hiddy

Jahan. Barrington, unexpectedly dismissed by Mohamed Yasin a year earlier, made the foxy little Pakistani pay a high price for that effrontery. Mohamed Asran effectively slowed the pace for a while against Mohibullah, and Ahmed Safwat led Alauddin 5-1; but neither Egyptian could resist the remorseless pressure imposed on him. Cam Nancarrow, who had been struggling to strike form, eventually seemed to do so as he emerged from a tough, disputatious, but often spectacular match with Torsam Khan.

In the quarters, Hunt and Barrington, the only men to win the title in the previous eight seasons, were swept aside by the Pakistanis. Alauddin played Barrington's game better, much better, and was never in trouble except for a brief spell in the second game. But Zaman's win over Hunt, who won the first two games and led 7-5 in the fifth, produced the best match and the outstanding individual performance of the championship. Zaman's game had long contained the seeds of greatness. They flowered now because of the patiently discreet self-discipline – and the precision – with which he exploited his enviable aptitude for the game. Azam Khan's training had done him good. He was still bold, but no longer reckless.

This was equally true of Jahan, who just managed to subdue Mohibullah. Jahan's natural aggression was always tempered by prudence. He was shrewd and accurate and made unusually good use of his cross-court backhand drop and his side-wall shots. He has seldom played better. Mohibullah had four chances to win the first game, and two chances to win the fourth: but he lost both. When it came to a crisis, he was over-excited and erratic. Ken Hiscoe came from behind to beat Nancarrow in the fifth game of a tempestuously lively match that ended with Nancarrow sliding about the court with only one shoe on. As a spectacle, it was rather like watching two powerful cars struggling for priority on a narrow road.

So Hiscoe was the only Australian in the last four – at the age of 37; after recovering from back trouble that threatened to end his career; and 13 years after reaching the semi-finals of the British amateur championship at his first attempt. His challenge to Alauddin was astute, aggressive, and tenacious, but he made a lot of mistakes. The nimble Alauddin played a smoothly and almost flawlessly designed game to beat him in 29 minutes.

Zaman was now looking every inch a champion. He lost only one game to Jahan, whose tribulations were aggravated by his angry reaction to Dick Hawkey's refereeing. Jahan was threatened with disqualification and he wanted the referee changed. But Zaman, always the deadpan humorist, caused a roar of laughter by

Qamar Zaman's expression tells everything – it is the smile of a man who has just won the British Open championship. The squash world belongs to Zaman . . . at least for the time being.

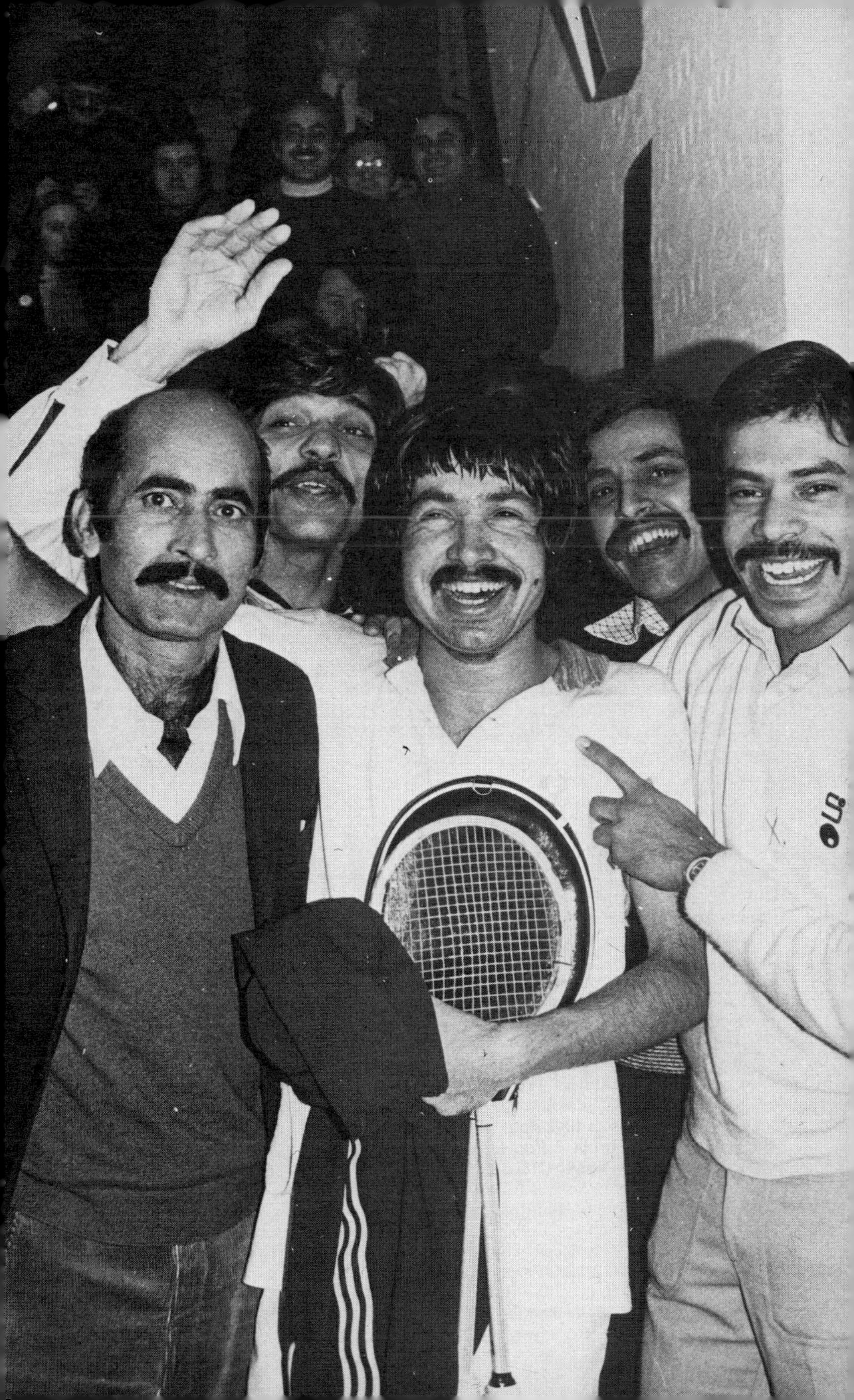

telling Hawkey he was 'a very good referee' (Zaman was leading 9-4 and 6-2 at the time). Jahan then put all the fuss behind him and in the third game played his best squash of the match – but in the end he was engulfed by a sparkling tide of winners.

If memory serves me right, neither Taleb nor any of the great Khans matched the flamboyant splendour with which Zaman won the final. He beat Alauddin 9-7, 9-6, 9-1 in 66 minutes, an astonishingly crushing result considering Alauddin's previous form. The imaginative versatility of Zaman's game prevented Alauddin from achieving the rhythm essential to his best form. In the second game Alauddin, teasing Zaman with lobs and backhand angles, led 6-4 and was going well. But a few lets broke the spell – and Alauddin scored only one more point in the match. The third game was an exhibition, with Zaman masking his shots delightfully against a now demoralised opponent.

So ended a memorable triumph by a player of bewildering charm – a triumph all the more remarkable because, throughout the championship, Zaman was having treatment to reduce the pain and swelling from an abscess on a wisdom tooth. It can be no comfort to anyone (except Zaman) that next season he should be 100 per cent fit . . .

OPEN RESULTS

FIRST ROUND

G. Hunt (Australia) bt D. Jackman (Australia) 9-3, 9-1, 9-1
M. Khalifa (Egypt) bt S. J. Khan (Pakistan) 9-0, 9-0, 9-2
K. Shawcross (Australia) bt N. Barbour (NZ) 9-6, 9-7, 7-9, 5-9, 9-5
W. Reedman (Australia) bt C. Booth (Australia) 9-1, 9-3, 9-2
Q. Zaman (Pakistan) bt A. Aziz (Egypt) 9-4, 9-4, 9-3
P. Millman (GB) w.o. B. Patterson (GB) scr.
A. Kaoud (Egypt) bt A. Rashid (Egypt) 9-4, 9-1, 9-5
P. Ayton (GB) bt K. Dowling (SA) 10-8, 9-1, 9-4
H. Jahan (Pakistan) bt K. Ibrahim (Egypt) 9-6, 9-7, 9-8
B. Brownlee (NZ) bt P. Chard (New Guinea) 9-3, 9-4, 9-10, 9-10, 9-7
J. Beattie (GB) bt B. Wise (GB) 9-0, 9-0, 9-1
J. Easter (GB) bt A. Swift (GB) 9-0, 9-2, 10-8
M. Khan (Pakistan) bt T. Connor (Australia) 9-1, 9-1, 9-1
M. Corby (GB) bt Z. Khan (Pakistan) 9-0, 9-1, 9-7
Rehmat Khan (Pakistan) bt T. Prateley (GB) 9-4, 9-5, 9-3
M. Asran (Egypt) bt T. Colyer (NZ) 9-3, 9-0, 9-3
M. Yasin (Pakistan) bt C. Francis (GB) 9-0, 9-4, 9-3
Abbas Khan (Pakistan) bt I. Din (India) 9-4, 9-6, 9-4
P. Wright (GB) bt W. Sabey (GB) 9-7, 4-9, 9-2, 9-4
J. Barrington (GB) bt K. Bruce-Lockhart (GB) 9-5, 9-2, 9-1
A. Safwat (Egypt) bt G. Allam (Egypt) 9-1, 9-1, 9-7
M. Nathanson (Sweden) bt H. Din (India) 9-4, 9-1, 9-5
J. Mabbit (GB) bt M. M'Fuk (Nigeria) 9-6, 9-2, 9-1

G. Alauddin (Pakistan) bt J. Richardson (GB) 9-0, 9-0, 9-1
M. Saleem (Pakistan) bt I. Robinson (GB) 9-3, 6-9, 10-8, 9-1
J. Leslie (GB) bt M. Hellstrom (Sweden) 9-5, 9-4, 9-5
Atlas Khan (Pakistan) bt Amanullah Khan (Pakistan) 9-5, 9-2, 9-4
K. Hiscoe (Australia) bt D. Goldson (GB) 9-1, 9-2, 9-5
T. Khan (Pakistan) bt M. Grundy (GB) 9-0, 9-4, 9-0
Rematullah Khan (Pakistan) bt C. Roe (GB) 9-2, 9-6, 9-3
E. Maasarani (Egypt) bt A. Nadi (Egypt) 9-2, 9-0, 9-0
C. Nancarrow (Australia) bt H. Colburn 9-5, 9-1, 9-0

SECOND ROUND
Hunt bt Khalifa 9-6, 9-0, 9-0
Reedman bt Shawcross 9-7, 7-9, 10-9, 9-2
Zaman bt Millman 9-1, 9-3, 9-6
Ayton bt Kaoud 10-8, 9-7, 9-1
Jahan bt Brownlee 7-9, 9-4, 9-5, 9-2
Easter bt Beattie 9-1, 9-1, 9-1
M. Khan bt Corby 9-1, 9-0, 9-2
Asran bt Rehmat Khan 9-2, 9-5, 9-4
Yasin bt Abbas Khan 9-3, 9-4, 9-6
Barrington bt Wright 9-0, 9-0, 9-1
Safwat bt Nathanson 9-7, 9-3, 9-6
Alauddin bt Mabbit 9-2, 9-7, 9-3
Saleem bt Leslie 9-1, 9-4, 10-9
Hiscoe bt Atlas Khan 9-2, 9-4, 9-2
T. Khan bt Rematullah Khan 6-9, 9-7, 9-0, 9-6
Nancarrow bt Maasarani 9-0, 9-3, 9-2

THIRD ROUND
Hunt bt Reedman 9-2, 9-0, 9-3
Zaman bt Ayton 2-9, 9-2, 9-0, 9-1
Jahan bt Easter 4-9, 9-5, 9-4, 9-4
M. Khan bt Asran 9-2, 5-9, 9-4, 9-2
Barrington bt Yasin 9-4, 9-3, 9-4
Alauddin bt Safwat 9-6, 9-1, 9-0
Hiscoe bt Saleem 9-3, 9-0, 9-5
Nancarrow bt T. Khan 3-9, 9-7, 10-8, 6-9, 9-0

QUARTER-FINALS
Zaman bt Hunt 4-9, 8-10, 9-3, 9-2, 9-7
Jahan bt Khan 10-8, 9-3, 7-9, 10-8
Alauddin bt Barrington 9-3, 9-6, 9-0
Hiscoe bt Nancarrow 9-4, 3-9, 6-9, 9-2, 9-6

SEMI-FINALS
Zaman bt Jahan 9-4, 9-2, 6-9, 9-4
Alauddin bt Hiscoe 9-3, 9-5, 9-5

THIRD PLACE PLAY-OFF
Hiscoe bt Jahan 9-5, 9-2, 8-10, 9-4

FINAL
Zaman bt Alauddin 9-7, 9-6, 9-1

CHICHESTER FESTIVAL

An eight-man professional tournam t was the hub of an ambitiously diversified seven- nt festival, sponsored by Slazenger, at the enterpris g Chichester club. In considering the best means of cele rating the acquisition of a new court (with a glass ba -wall), Chichester were torn between men and wome professionals and amateurs, stars and satellites, and, far as the format was concerned, knock-out or all-play- ll. Eventually they boldly went for the lot.

It was a pity that such a mass ly comprehensive promotion clashed with a professio l team event at Coventry and the men's amateur national series at Newport. But Chichester attract ong cosmopolitan field and the tournament was ably successful – though many players found the p gramming excessively arduous.

At first the professionals played ir o groups of four on an all-play-all basis. Torsam K n had the best record in one group, though Rehmat han managed to beat him in five. Cam Nancarrow was t at his sharpest. He took only eight points from Tors nd was stretched to five games by Mohamed Asran a Rehmat. Hiddy Jahan dominated the other group, and ly Bill Reedman could take a game from him. In vie of the congested schedule, it was to Jahan's later be t that he saved himself some hard labour by winning group matches so quickly. Ahmed Safwat was secon in this group, though he was taken to 9-7 in the fift by both Bryan Patterson (who almost beat him in thre and Reedman.

By this time even Safwat's enviable st k of energy was diminishing. But he came from behin o beat Torsam 8-10, 9-10, 9-4, 9-5, 10-8 in a thrilling nd spectacular semi-final, the best match of the tour ment. Torsam led 8-6 in the fifth, but Safwat was aw rded a let and made the most of his chance – bouncin ck in triumph from the brink of defeat. The effort fi d him. Jahan conceded only 13 points to Nancarrow in e other semi-final, and only 13 to Safwat in the final.

Jahan had lost only one game in his fo r matches on the way to the final, whereas Safwat h three times been taken to five and had run himself to the floor. Inevitably, there was now a clear dispari in physical and mental fitness, and there was a psych gical factor, too: Safwat had never beaten Jahan.

Even so, the first game was a reminder t t these two are among the game's most delightful shot makers and offer spectators the bonus of a sharp contr t in styles: with Jahan depending largely on reverberat g violence and Safwat on agility and touch. That g me was a beauty – and Safwat led 7-4. After that, he d nothing left, and we suddenly noticed that he could no longer spring back to mid-court after picking up Jahan's drops. Safwat was cooked.

This tournament was one of many to demonstrate Jahan's growing maturity as a match-player. The years have taught him discretion; he has learned to pace himself through a match, to pick his punches carefully instead of blasting away like a machine-gun. A feature of the final was the ease with which he read Safwat's game: Jahan played with an authority to match his proud bearing. Chichester was his third tournament final in nine days, but the first he had won.

RESULTS

SEMI-FINALS
A. Safwat bt T. Khan 8-10, 9-10, 9-4, 9-5, 10-8
H. Jahan bt C. Nancarrow 9-4, 9-4, 9-5

FINAL
H. Jahan bt A. Safwat 9-7, 9-3, 9-3

BRITISH CALEDONIAN AIRWAYS – YELLOW DOT GRAND PRIX

The most exciting innovation of a memorably eventful professional season was the eight-man grand prix circuit sponsored by British Caledonian Airways and Yellow Dot Sportswear. It ended with Geoff Hunt and Jonah Barrington, the only men to win the British open championship in the previous eight seasons, at opposite extremes of the earnings list – Hunt with £3,000, Barrington with only £775 (though most of us would consider that a reasonable reward for 15 days' work).

The grand prix was one of those rare promotional concepts that, from birth, are close to perfection. It consisted of five three-day tournaments, each carrying £1,875 in prize-money, with points allocations graded from 80 for the winner, down to 10 for whoever finished last. A bonus pool of £3,050 lifted the total 'up for grabs' to £12,425 – and thus led the professional game into the lushest pastures it had ever known.

In addition to the usual knockout, the losers went into a play-off series. This had two purposes. First, it meant that every tournament ended with the players ranked from one to eight (tournament prize-money and grand prix points were awarded accordingly). Second, it meant that every man played every night in a four-match programme.

In passing, it was ridiculous (except as evidence of widespread inflation) to add a zero to all the points awards. Nor was it necessary to give the eighth man any points at all. But those are criticisms of the format's application rather than its basic merit. Here was a system in which a man could lose in the first round and still earn £175 (and 40 grand prix points) by finishing fifth. It was hardly surprising that the play-off matches tended to be just as hotly contested and just as exciting as the others. Up to a point, they also tended to be just as distinguished – because the eight players were so evenly matched that the slightest fluctuations in form could plunge even Hunt into the play-offs. Indeed, Barrington and Torsam Khan were hardly ever in anything else, because they always lost on the first day.

The competitive pressures never relaxed. Win or lose, there was always plenty to play for the next evening. Failure was always relative, never final. A joyous by-product of this was the way the players went for their shots; they were seldom inhibited, and the result was gloriously spectacular squash in one match after another. In 'showing the flag' at Leicester, Edinburgh, Manchester, Newcastle, and Wembley in turn, the grand prix was therefore of immense value in polishing the image of the game as a whole and the professional game in particular. The galleries were usually packed (Edinburgh and Wembley were the least successful tournaments), and the spectators usually delighted.

It was not roses all the way, of course. Matches between Ken Hiscoe and Cam Nancarrow, for example, usually consist of a series of collisions, embraces, lets, and penalty points interrupted by lively and highly skilled squash – which is a minority taste. Torsam and Barrington, too, were sometimes guilty of conduct that fell below the standard we expect professionals to set. But for the most part all was sweetness and light, and even the 'villains' often made such exaggerated efforts to be nice to each other that it was like watching atheists at prayer.

Inevitably, those who look for a cloud beyond every silver lining trotted out the old argument that the emotional stress of playing for big money destroys the spirit of the game. It does nothing of the sort; it merely puts a man's character to the test. Anybody can be affable when there is little or nothing at stake, but put him under pressure and you soon find out how deeply his virtue is rooted.

Ahmed Safwat and Hiddy Jahan, strikingly handsome men, produced the most spectacular squash of the circuit and were also sufficiently good match-players to finish fourth and second respectively. Hunt, beaten only by Safwat and Gogi Alauddin, again displayed an astonishing capacity for maintaining peak form, or something very close to it, in a succession of tough matches. Alauddin spelt out the basics of squash with a silken ease that suggested no game could be easier. Nancarrow, short of match play and scratching for form, lost six successive matches before reminding us what he could do. Hiscoe, who had his 37th birthday on the first day of the circuit, gamely – and to a degree, effectively – struggled to forget it, but withdrew from his last match because his legs felt bad.

Torsam and Barrington had more problems than most. Their match at Leicester was a bad one and Torsam, intensely competitive and perhaps too eager to establish himself, was disputatious about rights of way. Barrington refused to shake hands and next day Torsam was ticked off by the tournament manager, the sponsors, and some of the players. Even the spectators got at him, but we could understand his behaviour, without excusing it; he was still learning his trade, and later he did make a big effort to discipline his bristling ambition. But the fuss doubtless affected him, and later, at Newcastle, measles forced him to retire from one match and scratch from another.

Barrington had been playing well. But during the grand prix so many things went wrong for him that he lost confidence and became dispirited. He missed his first match because his wife Madeleine, who was pregnant, had been rushed to hospital. Next day, against Torsam, his zest for the game seemed limited, and after that, he was always in trouble. At Wembley, he had to retire from his first match after collapsing with acute respiratory problems. The next evening, a Nancarrow follow-through clipped him by the right eye and there was a 10-minute 'blood break'. That left Barrington with restricted vision and an ugly wound, so by that time he must have felt reasonably sure that, whatever happened next, he was not going to enjoy it.

Six men went straight into the grand prix and Safwat (who beat Rehmat Khan and Bill Reedman) and Torsam (he handled Abbas Kaoud and Mohamed Asran) emerged from a severe qualifying competition at Durham. Each made an impressive contribution to the grand prix. But for that attack of measles, Torsam might have finished sixth instead of seventh, yet he had his troubles at Leicester and we could never be sure when the volcano was going to erupt again.

Hunt did not lose a game at Leicester, where Jahan's forehand left dents in the tin. Alauddin took over the lead by winning Edinburgh (Safwat came back from 3-8 down in the fifth to beat Hunt), but there was no stopping Hunt at Manchester, where Nancarrow disposed of Alauddin and – in a wildly fluctuating match – Jahan. By this time Alauddin, Jahan, and Safwat were neck and neck in second place, with Barrington, Nancarrow, and Torsam also in a bunch some way behind them, and Hiscoe puffing and snorting on their heels. The jockeying for position was boisterous.

Hunt beat Jahan in the Newcastle final; but at Wembley he had to yield to Alauddin, who then beat Jahan in the final. The bothered and battered Barrington finished last – and did his reputation no good with his tetchy and often ungracious loquacity in the ultimate play-off. Wembley was more of an anti-climax than a climax. The galleries were not of a kind to stimulate players who were obviously jaded, and one felt that on a circuit of this kind, five tournaments were probably enough. Three weeks later Qamar Zaman and Mohibullah Khan turned professional, which meant that (if the format remained unchanged) the 1975–76 grand prix would be even tougher.

The final placings contained one oddity in that, although Jahan finished second on points and earned a larger bonus, Alauddin won £75 more, overall, because he secured the £500 first prize at both Edinburgh and Wembley.

GRAND PRIX SUMMARY

Position	*Player*	*Points*	*Bonus* (£)	*Tournament prize-money* (£)	*Total earnings* (£)
1	Hunt	360	1,000	2,000	3,000
2	Jahan	310	650	1,450	2,100
3	Alauddin	290	500	1,675	2,175
4	Safwat	240	325	1,100	1,425
5	Nancarrow	180	200	975	1,175
6	Hiscoe	160	150	775	925
7	Torsam	140	125	725	850
8	Barrington	120	100	675	775

FIRST LEG; *at Squash Leicester, 21–23 January*
1 Hunt; 2 Alauddin; 3 Jahan; 4 Safwat; 5 Hiscoe; 6 Torsam Khan; 7 Barrington; 8 Nancarrow.

SECOND LEG; *at Edinburgh Sports Club, 13–15 February*
1 Alauddin; 2 Safwat; 3 Hunt; 4 Jahan; 5 Barrington; 6 Hiscoe; 7 Torsam Khan; 8 Nancarrow.

THIRD LEG; *at Northern LT & SC, Manchester, 17–19 February*
1 Hunt; 2 Nancarrow; 3 Jahan; 4 Safwat; 5 Torsam Khan; 6 Barrington; 7 Alauddin; 8 Hiscoe.

FOURTH LEG; *at Squash Newcastle, 7–9 March*
1 Hunt; 2 Jahan; 3 Nancarrow; 4 Safwat; 5 Alauddin; 6 Hiscoe; 7 Barrington; 8 Torsam Khan.

FINAL LEG; *at Wembley SC, 16–18 March*
1 Alauddin; 2 Jahan; 3 Hunt; 4 Hiscoe; 5 Torsam Khan; 6 Nancarrow; 7 Safwat; 8 Barrington.

PROFESSIONAL TEAM SERIES

A bold and imaginative addition to the professional season was a two-man team series in which Gogi Alauddin and Jonah Barrington beat Ken Hiscoe and Geoff Hunt by nine matches to five. It was bold because the players and their agents took the plunge without the security of a sponsor. It was imaginative because the format was new to squash, though it was an exact replica of that used in Davis Cup tennis matches – with two singles on the first day, a doubles on the second, and the reverse singles on the third day.

The prize-money depended on the gate. The galleries were mostly so good that, after all the costs had been met, the players had about £1,800 to share. As the series occupied a total of eight days on three successive weekends in January, it was also a usefully rigorous preparation for the British Open championship. The wider significance of this successful innovation was its value as a prototype for what could be a genuine international professional team championship; initially, this would probably feature Pakistan, Australia, Egypt, and Britain.

In this respect last season's series had an obvious weakness in that Alauddin and Barrington were not a national team. But the only real cause for concern was the doubles. This exciting and unfamiliar form of the game, doubly unfamiliar because the American scoring system was used, with a point awarded for every rally, provided some lively entertainment. But the lack of doubles courts led to congestion on the smaller singles courts. There was evidence, too, that a day's programme consisting solely of a doubles match was not enough to attract the public in sufficient numbers. At Wembley, the doubles was cancelled because ticket sales would not have justified hiring the court.

The Australians lost the series because Hiscoe could win only one game in six singles, because Alauddin beat Hunt at Abbeydale Park, and because Alauddin and Barrington came from behind to win the doubles at Brandon Hall.

At Abbeydale, form was uncertain. We knew Barrington was playing well, but the others had been in England less than a week. The series had a thrilling start when Alauddin beat the erratic Hunt in five; and Barrington also stretched Hunt to five. In the fourth game Barrington took a bang in the face but had a run of eight points out of nine. He was too negative at the start of the fifth and

Hunt went to 5-0, which was just too much for Barrington to make up.

The Australians turned 0-3 into 2-3 before leaving Abbeydale, and they lost by the same margin at Coventry. Alauddin had to pay a high price for whipping Hunt 9-0 in an eight-minute first game – the first rally lasted two minutes. Hiscoe briefly got to grips with Barrington. The doubles was a setback for the Australians, for had they won it, the series would have been levelled at 5-5. As it was, they went to Wembley 4-6 down.

The players were all jaded by then (especially Hiscoe), because they went to Wembley straight from a grand prix tournament at Leicester. Hunt beat Alauddin for the second time in less than 24 hours, but Barrington and Alauddin in turn firmly dealt with Hiscoe to settle the series. Then the event ended as it began, with Hunt losing a dramatic match in five games. This time it was Barrington who handled him, for the first time since 1972. Two games down, Hunt won the third and fourth and went to 2-0 in the fifth without making a single mistake. This astonishing burst ended when he hit a backhand boast down – and Barrington scored five points in one hand to regain control of a match that delighted connoisseurs and casual spectators alike.

Rex Bellamy is squash and tennis correspondent for The Times.

DURHAM OPEN

(by Jeff Todhunter)

This was surely the match of the season: Qamar Zaman, who had beaten Geoff Hunt *en route* to the British Open title, confirmed his status as world No. 1 by defeating the Australian again in their first encounter since Wembley. Hunt's defeat came in the semi-final of the Durham and Teesside Open championships at Stockton YMCA (8–12 February) where Zaman went on to win the title by beating fellow Pakistani Mohibullah Khan.

The final was a fine match (reversing the result of the British Amateur final), but the semi-final was unforgettable. Hunt had vowed revenge; Zaman was determined to maintain his status; and both players poured their hearts into a brilliant 82-minute five-setter, to make a match that only great players could have produced.

Hunt, three times Durham champion, moved the Pakistani rapidly round court and, as Zaman missed more than a few drop shots, took the first game 9-1 in 10 minutes. But the Open champion shook his game together and 20 minutes later was 2-1 up. He stepped up the pace, and Hunt was powerless against a stream of drop shots, nicks, and wrong-footing drives, backed up by incredible fleetness of foot. However, Hunt took the fourth with great courage. A long, gasping rally at 3-2 had both men stretching like contortionists, which took much out of both of them; but Hunt somehow found the strength to maintain pressure for five points, and suddenly it was two-all.

The deciding set lasted a noble 37 minutes. But the long, excitingly competitive rallies sapped the Australian as Zaman, his amazing mobility seemingly unimpaired, ran him around cruelly. Hunt was forced to stretch more and more under the merciless pressure; Herculean effort saved two match points, but he was powerless against the third. He left the court ashen-faced with tiredness.

Zaman's final against Mohibullah was a quicksilver affair, with incredible retrieving that Zaman controlled – just – once he had thrown off the hangover from the Hunt match. But it was a hard 103-minute battle that was decided only by the marginal difference in mobility.

RESULTS

QUARTER-FINALS
G. Hunt bt S. Muneer 9-6, 9-1, 9-4
Q. Zaman bt K. Hiscoe 9-3, 9-0, 9-6
A. Safwat bt C. Nancarrow 9-7, 9-4, 9-0
M. Khan bt T. Khan 9-2, 9-1, 9-0

SEMI-FINALS
Zaman bt Hunt 1-9, 9-4, 9-2, 2-9, 9-5
M. Khan bt Safwat 9-2, 10-9, 9-3

THIRD PLACE PLAY-OFF
Hunt bt Safwat 9-4, 7-9, 1-9, 9-7, 9-3

FINAL
Zaman bt M. Khan 7-9, 9-4, 9-6, 9-6

ROLEX NORTH WEST OPEN
6–12 January, Preston
Q. Zaman bt H. Jahan 9-4, 5-9, 10-8, 9-0

WARRINGTON OPEN
10–15 March, Warrington
Final Geoff Hunt bt Gogi Alauddin 9-4, 6-9, 5-9, 9-4, 10-8
Third place play-off K. Hiscoe bt C. Nancarrow 9-4, 4-9, 9-7, 5-9, 8-0 (Nancarrow retd)

HARP LAGER TROPHY
15 April, Wembley
B. Patterson bt M. Khalifa Salim 9-6, 9-5, 10-8

IRELAND 1974–75

Declan Hassett & Owen Wilson

The Irish squad could not have had a better preparation for the European Championships, the climax to a hectic home season. John McGrath, the captain, applied himself assiduously to the task of bringing his side to a competitive peak; tangible evidence of his dedication was seen as far back as September when he competed in an open tournament at Waterford, along with Ben Cranwell and Bernard O'Gorman.

O'Gorman there achieved his only win over the player from the Windsor club in Belfast; for McGrath went on to enjoy a tremendous season, taking the Irish Closed and winning all his matches for Ulster in the inter-provincials in Dublin in January.

New Zealander Cranwell was the powerhouse in the Leinster club's bid for the all-Ireland club title – they lost to Fitzwilliam in the final – and he won an Ulster open title in Belfast.

O'Gorman, a full-time coach with the Squash Ireland organisation, was laid low by illness prior to the start of the inter-provincials. He was beaten by Munster open champion Val Flanagan in the opening match, then collapsed against McGrath, but recovered in time to help Fitzwilliam to victory.

Bob Weir played a few matches in Ireland but concentrated his preparations on the British club circuit.

Gerry Doherty of Ulster, now living in Dublin after a few years abroad, appeared in the team that beat Munster and Leinster in pre-Christmas matches, and in the North of Ireland side that took the inter-pro title from Leinster.

Donal Byrne was one of the more experienced players in the squad and his tussles with the rising young star from the north, David Gotto, produced some great squash.

In the triangular internationals at Newport, Ireland went down to England as expected, but had a tremendous win over Scotland who had beaten them in the European championships in 1973 and 1974.

Big money (£1,900) for the Dunlop Irish Open attracted big names in the professional game, with the exception of Geoff Hunt, the holder. Hunt did not compete because of a dispute over a contribution towards his air fare from Australia. It will never be known if Hunt would have retained his title, but Gogi Alauddin's dismissal of his compatriot Hiddy Jahan in straight games in the final was a disappointing climax to four days of very mixed squash. Cam Nancarrow filled third spot at the expense of the volatile Torsam Khan. A popular winner of the plate was John Easter, who had been contracted that weekend to help the Irish squad in their preparation for the European event.

The Irish women showed their undoubted class in the triangular internationals staged at Cork during January. They swept through unbeaten against Wales and Scotland, dropping just two games. Geraldine Barniville won the top match of the series against the Collington Castle player Brenda Carmichael, showing supreme quality of stroke-play.

Last season the Irish women also met England for the first time in Ireland, and did better than the 4–1 scoreline suggests. Dorothy Armstrong beat Barbara Diggens at No. 3, and an Irish victory was possible in the second match when Irene Hewitt led Fran Marshall 2–1 – but Mrs Marshall broke back and took the match 9–6 in the fifth. Stephanie Lynas went to five against Pat Francis, losing the decider 7–9.

ULSTER OPEN (men)

John McGrath's absence (at the British Amateur) and the emergence of David Gotto were significant factors. It was the second year that McGrath had missed the event and Gotto took the chance to establish himself with wins over senior players Peter Ledbetter and Bernard O'Gorman.

In the final he was halted by Ben Cranwell, the latter putting on a convincing display of percentage squash. Cranwell proved himself the better tactician throughout, keeping Gotto on the move with raking drives and delicate drop shots. Cranwell's 9–7, 9–7, 9–2 win was the first by a Leinster player since 1967.

IRISH CLOSED

John McGrath retained his title with a 10–8, 9–1, 9–1 win over O'Gorman. The first game was the crucial one; initially O'Gorman was the steadier of the two, and established leads of 5–1 and 7–4. But he failed to use his advantage, and McGrath's greater incisiveness allowed him back into the match. From the second game onwards McGrath was firmly in control and he took the final game in only six minutes.

ULSTER WOMEN'S CLOSED

Though this was a new event, it produced finalists of long standing – Dorothy Armstrong and Stephanie Lynas.

The pair provided an epic struggle, Dorothy being No. 1 in Ulster and her opponent No. 2 – positions that were reversed after the final.

Stephanie won 9–6, 3–9, 9–1, 9–6 and generally looked the fitter player. She was able to sustain pressure, and eventually wore Dorothy down.

IRISH WOMEN'S OPEN

The entry could not have been bettered: from England came that seemingly ageless competitor Fran Marshall, who was made No. 1; from Dublin came Geraldine Barniville, the holder and No. 2 seed; while two Irish exiles, Irene Hewitt and Barbara Sanderson, filled up places three and four.

Barbara was surprisingly beaten in the quarter-finals, going down in straight games to No. 5 Dorothy Armstrong. She never seemed to be in the match and won only five points. Dorothy found Fran's experience and expertise too much for her in the semi-finals, and lost 3–1 in an exciting finish. In the other semi-final, Irene looked as though she was going to streak away with the match when she led Geraldine 2–0. But Geraldine rallied well and Irene was thankful to come home 9–6 in the fifth.

By taking the final 9–7, 9–2, 1–9, 10–8 Fran won her first Irish Open title. She trailed 3–6 in the fourth game, but with a series of winning drops, both straight and crosscourt, overhauled her opponent for a deserved victory.

RESULTS

MEN

Irish Closed J. McGrath bt B. O'Gorman 3-0
Ulster Open Handicap D. Doherty bt G. Hull 2-1
Ulster Open B. Cranwell bt D. Gotto 3-0
Guinness Trophy J. McGrath bt D. Gotto 3-0
C.I.Y.M.S. Invitation J. McGrath bt D. Gotto 3-1
Ulster Intermediate Closed A. Derry bt B. Murray 3-0
Ulster Junior J. Kane bt K. Lucas 3-0

WOMEN

Irish Open F. Marshall bt I. Hewitt 3-1
Ulster Open Handicap D. Armstrong bt C. McNeice 2-1
Ulster Closed S. Lynas bt D. Armstrong 3-1
Guinness Trophy D. Armstrong bt J. Morrison 3-0
Ulster Intermediate A. McCartney bt C. McNeice 3-2
Ulster Junior J. Bassett bt J. Orr 3-0
All-Ireland Team Windsor bt Lisburn 3-2

SOUTH AFRICA 1974

Owen Emslie

PROFESSIONAL CIRCUIT

Every year the professional circuit in South Africa has grown. 1974 was no exception, with a record sponsorship of £14,500. Only three Pakistanis – Gogi Alauddin, Mohibullah Khan, and Qamar Zaman – were missing out of the world's top eight players, which reflected the quality of entry.

The circuit began with the Rennie's South African Open, which was an unqualified success. The tournament was a sell-out from the first round and the crowds had the match court at the University of Witwatersrand bursting at the seams.

All the seeds won through to the quarter-finals, the match between Ahmed Safwat and Graham Macdonald delighting the spectators. Both players used the angle to such an extent that the boring drive down the side wall was temporarily forgotten. Safwat won in four. The only other seeds to be extended were Ken Hiscoe, at No. 5, who dropped a game to Dave Quail, and John Easter, at No. 6, who beat Doug Barrow in four.

Geoff Hunt met unexpected resistance from Roland Watson in their quarter-final match. Watson played well above himself, keeping Hunt on the court for 80 minutes in the four games. Jonah Barrington had no such trouble, being far too steady for Hiscoe and winning in straight games. The explosive Hiddy Jahan crunched John Easter 9-1 in six minutes, lost control as Easter brilliantly re-asserted himself to take the second game, and then recovered to end victorious.

Once again it was Safwat who treated the crowd to an exhibition of squash artistry. His downfall is that he is often too adventurous, and when the occasion calls for care he will still go for his shots. His attitude makes for great entertainment but did not prove fruitful against the Australian Cam Nancarrow, who won after conceding the first game to Safwat.

The Hunt versus Barrington clash in the semi-finals was typical of their numerous encounters, with Hunt the aggressor and Barrington intent on extending the match for as long as possible. Hunt won in four after 85 minutes, while Jahan almost sprinted to victory over Nancarrow, blasting his opponent in 35 minutes with a truly amazing display of power squash.

When Jahan played Hunt, he tried to begin where he had ended against Nancarrow. He ran up a 4-0 lead, and then Hunt found a rhythm and no matter how well Jahan played he could not stave off defeat.

With the Open behind them, the seven visiting professionals, plus Roland Watson, began a five tournament circuit that took them to Durban, East London, Port Elizabeth, Cape Town, and Salisbury. The format for each tournament was to divide the players into two groups of four, each group playing a round robin and two leading players from each going forward to the semi-finals. The circuit proved to be a personal triumph for Hunt, as he won every event.

First stop was Durban, at the magnificent Cabana Beach courts in Umhlanga Rocks. The four finalists were Hunt, Nancarrow, Barrington, and Jahan.

Hunt played some erratic squash before he settled to his customary form to beat Jahan in five. Barrington and Nancarrow provided an incredible display. There was a let in the first rally and for the next hour and 40 minutes the two players mauled, bumped, and barged their way through five games. At one stage Barrington, in a fit of anger, rapped Nancarrow across the back with his racket. Nancarrow retaliated later by deliberately colliding with Barrington carrying him halfway across the court. The Australian eventually won 10-8 in the fifth.

In the final, Hunt completely outplayed Nancarrow, dropping only seven points in the process; while Jahan had a similar straight game revenge win over Barrington.

The round robin section of the Anglo American international was played in East London with the semi-finals and finals in Port Elizabeth. It proved to be a tournament of upsets. First Barrington dropped out through illness, giving Watson a walkover; then Nancarrow suffered two surprise reverses at the hands of Safwat and Watson. This latter pair won through to the semi-finals where they faced the inevitable Hunt and Jahan who had not dropped a game in their progress.

Hunt gained a predictable victory when he met Jahan in the final, but the third place play-off was remarkable for a fine recovery by Safwat. The Egyptian lost the first 15 points to Watson before winning in five.

The De Beers international was played in Cape Town, with Hunt and Nancarrow contesting the final. Here Nancarrow produced his best squash of the tour but it was still not good enough to beat Hunt. In the third place play-off Barrington accounted for Jahan in less than half an hour.

Watson found the form he had shown on the East coast when the circuit returned to Johannesburg for the Cygnet international. He beat both Safwat and Jahan, while in the other group John Easter gained his solitary victory, against Nancarrow. The final saw Hunt displaying his complete mastery of Barrington, while Watson did very well to take third spot at the expense of Ken Hiscoe.

For the final tournament the players were able to enjoy the magnificent facilities of the Salisbury Sports Club in Salisbury. The match court, especially built for the tournament circuit, can hold close to 1,000 spectators.

Hunt and Nancarrow qualified from their group, but the tour ended on a sad note for Easter – he lost to Rhodesian Steve Sherren, Watson's replacement for this event.

In the other group Barrington, Hiscoe, and Jahan had each won two matches but Hiscoe was edged out by the number of games against him. Hunt and Jahan eventually contested the final with the inevitable result, while Barrington let slip a chance for revenge over Nancarrow by losing the play-off.

THE AMATEUR SCENE

SYRRETS SA AMATEUR

Britain's Philip Ayton won his second South African title when he beat Selwyn Machet in straight games. The championships were played at the new complex at the Southern Suburbs Sports Club which boasted Johannesburg's first glass back-wall court.

Ayton, seeded No. 1, lost only one game during the championship – to Dawie Botha in the semi-finals. Selwyn Machet had one of the best wins of his career in the semi-finals when he defeated South African captain and twice holder of the title, Doug Barrow, in four pulsating games.

TRANSVAAL OPEN

Roland Watson firmly established himself as South Africa's leading player by winning the Transvaal Open for the second year running.

The quarter-finals provided three thrillers. Dave Scott came back from a 2-1 deficit to beat Alan Colburn after saving seven match points. Doug Barrow recovered from the same position to beat Melvyn Watson; and Selwyn Machet won in five against Philip Timperley after leading 2-0. Roland Watson beat fellow Springbok Dave Quail in the remaining quarter-final.

Watson won through to the finals with a comfortable straight game win over Machet, but Dave Scott notched up a fine victory over Doug Barrow.

Although Watson won in straight games, the final was a tremendous tussle, with Scott prepared to play all his shots and Watson relying on his phenomenal retrieving and experience to pull him through.

CHAMPION OF CHAMPIONS

The final tournament in the South African squash calendar, the Old Johannians Champion of Champions tournament, brought a new name to the list of winners of South Africa's major tournaments – Alan Colburn. Seeded six, he disposed of Dave Quail (No. 3) in the quarter-finals, Selwyn Machet (No. 2) in the semi-finals, and then had a great win over Dawie Botha in the final. The score of 9-5, 9-10, 2-9, 9-3, 9-2 showed Colburn's ascendancy over Botha in the last two games.

WP CINZANO CHAMPIONSHIP

The Western Province Open took on a new look with Cinzano as the sponsors. Former Springbok Derek Broom, who went into semi-retirement several years ago when he started farming, was in the draw at No. 2 with fellow Springbok, Keith Coppin, seeded at No. 1.

British player Ian Robinson, a late entry, was unseeded; but he eliminated No. 3 'J.P.' van Niekerk, to record the only upset in the quarter-finals.

In the semi-finals, Derek Becker caused a major upset by beating Keith Coppin in four entertaining games. Derek Broom played superlative squash, beating Robinson in straight games. Broom eventually won the title by beating Derek Becker in straight games, both players regularly hitting the nick.

WOMEN'S SQUASH

The disappointing aspect of women's squash in South Africa is the dearth of new young players of any standard. As in the past, 1974 found all the established players again being on top and, unfortunately, not being challenged by the youngsters. However Kathy Hardy, Jill Eckstein, and Gay Erskine would probably rank in the top five players in the world (excluding that Australian dynamo Heather McKay) so perhaps the juniors have a tough job on their hands.

In Rhodesia particularly, but also in the Western Province, Eastern Province, and Natal, there are a few hopes in the schoolgirl category, and one can only hope that they continue with the improvement that they have shown thus far.

Kathy Hardy again proved to be the best player. Although her performances in the lesser tournaments leave much to be desired, she becomes inspired when the 'big ones' come along and invariably comes out on top.

RESULTS (WOMEN)

SOUTH AFRICAN CHAMPIONSHIPS

QUARTER-FINALS
K. Hardy bt J. Donaldson 9-6, 9-5, 9-5
J. Eckstein bt D. Allen 9-5, 9-3, 9-6
G. Erskine bt T. Lawes 5-9, 9-7, 9-4, 9-2
S. Cogswell bt I. Hewitt 9-4, 9-5, 9-7

SEMI-FINALS
K. Hardy bt S. Cogswell 3-9, 10-9, 9-4, 9-2
G. Erskine bt J. Eckstein 10-8, 9-6, 4-9, 10-8

FINAL
K. Hardy bt G. Erskine 9-4, 6-9, 9-1, 10-9

CHAMPION OF CHAMPIONS

SEMI-FINALS
J. Eckstein bt G. Erskine 9-0, 9-6, 10-8
K. Hardy bt I. Hewitt 5-9, 9-6, 9-5, 9-5

FINAL
K. Hardy bt J. Eckstein 9-10, 10-9, 9-4, 10-9

RESULTS OF SOUTH AFRICAN CIRCUIT

McCARTHY LEYLAND SQUASH INTERNATIONAL – DURBAN

RED GROUP
Hunt bt Nancarrow 9-4, 9-2, 3-9, 9-5
Hunt bt Hiscoe 3-9, 9-0, 9-3, 6-9, 9-5
Hunt bt Safwat 9-10, 9-3, 9-7, 9-6
Nancarrow bt Hiscoe 8-10, 1-9, 9-0, 9-0, 9-6
Nancarrow bt Safwat 9-5, 8-10, 2-9, 9-3, 9-5
Hiscoe bt Safwat 3-9, 9-1, 4-9, 9-1, 10-9

BLUE GROUP
Jahan bt Easter 3-9, 9-3, 10-9, 9-1
Jahan bt Watson 9-7, 6-9, 9-6, 9-2
Barrington bt Jahan 1-9, 9-1, 9-10, 9-0, 9-3
Barrington bt Easter 9-7, 9-4, 9-5
Barrington bt Watson 10-9, 9-2, 9-2
Watson bt Easter 9-10, 9-3, 3-9, 9-2, 9-3

SEMI-FINALS
Hunt bt Jahan 6-9, 9-1, 2-9, 9-1, 9-2
Nancarrow bt Barrington 7-9, 9-4, 2-9, 9-4, 10-8

THIRD PLACE PLAY-OFF
Jahan bt Barrington 9-7, 9-7, 10-8

FINAL
Hunt bt Nancarrow 9-5, 9-2, 9-0

ANGLO AMERICAN SQUASH INTERNATIONAL – EAST LONDON/PORT ELIZABETH

RED GROUP
Hunt bt Jahan 10-8, 9-4, 9-1
Hunt bt Hiscoe 10-9, 9-6, 9-6
Hunt bt Easter 9-3, 10-8, 9-6
Jahan bt Hiscoe 6-9, 10-8, 9-5, 7-9, 9-3
Jahan bt Easter 9-4, 9-7, 9-7
Hiscoe bt Easter 9-7, 0-9, 9-7, 3-9, 9-0

BLUE GROUP
Nancarrow bt Barrington 5-9, 9-1, 9-0, 9-0
Barrington bt Safwat 9-2, 3-9, 9-2, 9-7
Watson bt Nancarrow 1-9, 9-3, 9-1, 10-8
Watson bt Barrington 9-0, 9-0, 9-0
Safwat bt Nancarrow 9-4, 5-9, 9-7, 9-5
Safwat bt Watson 9-5, 7-9, 9-4, 10-9

SEMI-FINALS
Hunt bt Safwat 9-4, 9-4, 10-8
Jahan bt Watson 9-6, 10-8, 9-10, 9-3

THIRD PLACE PLAY-OFF
Safwat bt Watson 0-9, 6-9, 9-6, 9-6, 9-0

FINAL
Hunt bt Jahan 9-5, 9-3, 9-5

DE BEERS SQUASH INTERNATIONAL – CAPE TOWN

RED GROUP
Jahan bt Watson 9-4, 7-9, 9-3, 10-8
Jahan bt Hiscoe 9-2, 3-9, 9-5, 10-9
Jahan bt Barrington 9-5, 9-6, 9-7
Watson bt Hiscoe 9-1, 5-9, 9-7, 10-8
Barrington bt Watson 4-9, 9-5, 9-0, 9-3
Barrington bt Hiscoe 4-9, 7-9, 9-4, 9-3, 9-0

BLUE GROUP
Hunt bt Safwat 9-4, 9-2, 9-7
Hunt bt Nancarrow 7-9, 1-9, 9-4, 9-1, 9-4
Hunt bt Easter 9-7, 8-10, 10-9, 9-5
Nancarrow bt Safwat 9-6, 9-7, 9-5
Nancarrow bt Easter 9-7, 10-9, 9-5
Easter bt Safwat 9-3, 4-9, 9-4, 9-6

SEMI-FINALS
Hunt bt Barrington 10-8, 9-3, 1-9, 9-5
Nancarrow bt Jahan 9-6, 9-4, 5-9, 3-9, 9-5

THIRD PLACE PLAY-OFF
Barrington bt Jahan 9-3, 9-4, 9-1

FINAL
Hunt bt Nancarrow 7-9, 9-1, 9-5, 9-7

CYGNET SQUASH INTERNATIONAL – JOHANNESBURG

RED GROUP
Hunt bt Jahan 9-3, 9-6, 9-5
Hunt bt Watson 9-2, 9-0, 9-0
Hunt bt Safwat 9-4, 9-5, 10-8
Jahan bt Safwat 8-10, 9-7, 6-9, 10-8, 9-2
Watson bt Jahan 9-3, 9-5, 9-7
Watson bt Safwat 5-9, 9-0, 9-0, 9-4

BLUE GROUP
Barrington bt Nancarrow 5-9, 10-9, 9-7, 9-5
Barrington bt Easter 9-0, 9-4, 9-3
Barrington bt Hiscoe 9-3, 9-4, 9-4
Easter bt Nancarrow 9-5, 9-1, 9-1
Hiscoe bt Nancarrow 4-9, 9-4, 3-9, 9-7, 9-7
Hiscoe bt Easter 9-3, 9-3, 9-2

SEMI-FINALS
Hunt bt Hiscoe 10-8, 9-0, 9-1
Barrington bt Watson 9-1, 9-1, 6-9, 9-4

THIRD-PLACE PLAY-OFF
Watson bt Hiscoe 10-8, 9-0, 9-1

FINAL
Hunt bt Barrington 9-2, 9-4, 9-7

RENNIES SOUTH AFRICAN OPEN CHAMPIONSHIP

THIRD ROUND
G. Hunt bt S. Machet 9-0, 9-2, 9-2
R. Watson bt A. Colburn 9-5, 9-7, 9-5
J. Barrington bt D. Botha 9-3, 9-1, 9-6
K. Hiscoe bt D. Quail 9-4, 8-10, 9-0, 9-7
J. Easter bt D. Barrow 9-7, 3-9, 9-0, 9-3
H. Jahan bt D. Scott 9-2, 9-4, 9-1
A. Safwat bt G. Macdonald 9-4, 10-8, 6-9, 9-4
C. Nancarrow bt K. Coppin 9-7, 9-5, 10-9

QUARTER-FINALS
G. Hunt bt R. Watson 9-3, 6-9, 9-1, 9-4
J. Barrington bt K. Hiscoe 9-5, 9-6, 9-1
H. Jahan bt J. Easter 9-1, 3-9, 9-5, 9-6
C. Nancarrow bt A. Safwat 6-9, 9-5, 10-8, 10-8

SEMI-FINALS
G. Hunt bt J. Barrington 9-4, 9-7, 0-9, 9-4
H. Jahan bt C. Nancarrow 9-1, 9-6, 9-5

THIRD PLACE PLAY-OFF
C. Nancarrow bt J. Barrington 9-6, 6-9, 9-7, 4-9, 9-6

FINAL
G. Hunt bt H. Jahan 9-7, 9-7, 9-1

AUSTRALIA 1974

Robert Jolly

Australian squash has lost none of the expansionist virility for which it was noted throughout the sixties. Nowhere is this more clearly illustrated than in the northern state of Queensland.

The traditional power-houses of Australian squash have been the cities of Melbourne and Sydney, and thus the states Victoria and New South Wales. But in the past four or five years the vast area within the bounds of Queensland has been successfully harnessed by the administration to make it the most decentralised squash state in the nation, with the largest number of players competing on a weekly basis.

On top of the upsurge in squash in the north, the state is also enjoying for the first time being the holder of nearly all the national amateur championships titles. Queensland's haul at the last Australian Championships in 1974, was wins in the inter-state team events of senior men, women, and junior girls. Players featuring in the headlines were top national rankings Mike Donnelly and Dave Wright, and Marion Jackman, Jenny Irving, and Lyle Hubinger. Marion Jackman won the Australian Women's Championship, whilst another Queenslander, Rhonda Shapland, followed in her footsteps by taking the Australian junior crown.

The basis for all this success is best reflected in the growth of the game at the grassroots level. In 1970 there were 928 teams and 52 clubs affiliated to the SRA of Queensland. In four years these figures increased by 40% and 57% respectively to reveal a total of 1,627 teams and 129 clubs. And the courts keep going up.

With their former leading players turning to professional squash, the metropolises of Melbourne and Sydney are shifting the emphasis of top competition squash to include overseas players, and introducing a more substantial financial inducement. There were tours by Zaman and Mohibullah last year, during which the youngsters helped themselves to several state amateur titles, and Jahan and Alauddin raided the professional purses of the season's two major tournaments of international stature.

Australia's own golden boy of squash, Geoff Hunt,

Cam Nancarrow struggled to find his forn in Britain but the tenacious Aussie is never an easy opponent. His approach epitomises the determined Australian attitude to the game.

Australian women players lead the world Heather McKay is the by-word, but there is added strength with personalities such as Sue Newman (left) and Marion Jackman.

won both the invitation World Open championship in Melbourne on his home courts, and the Australian Professional Championship in Adelaide.

Open squash championships are flourishing despite the absence of a single sponsor of the size of the leaders in the UK circuit. The Australian Open (held in the nation's capital, Canberra), the New South Wales Open, the Coca Cola Open in Adelaide, and the Monash Open all registered successes. Wherever Hunt competed he collected first prize, despite determined challenges from local stars such as Leo Keppell, Ray Lewis, Tyson Burgess, Doug Stephensen, and Tony Hosford. The more familiar international names of Reedman, Nancarrow, and Hiscoe also failed to conquer Hunt's invincibility on his domestic circuit.

The key to the future expansion of the open competition will be the result of coordinated promotions and the benevolence of television, which carries solid doses of the sport into the living rooms of the population at regular intervals.

With the abdication of the top players into the professional ranks, the passage to the head of the amateur seedings has been eased considerably. This has been opportune in the development of the great talent Mike Donnelly, who is currently seeded above his old rival Dave Wright. The encouragement given by the SRA of Australia to the young players, who have grown out of the junior ranks, has been seen to have paid off in Donnelly's case. The institution of Under 23 touring teams in 1971 came at exactly the right time to stimulate talents such as Donnelly's. Ahead of him in the senior ranks were the foremost amateurs in the world at that time – Hunt, Hiscoe, Nancarrow and Carter. Donnelly's trips to New Zealand and South Africa not only gave him encouragement, but experience and maturity. The results are now being demonstrated admirably.

The Australian SRA is quite rightly pursuing the Under 23 teams, and versions of them, to widen the international experience of players just on the perimeter of the senior national teams. The women's association is healthy too. Once again the strong grassroots appeal of the game has led to considerable prowess at the international level, where the nation stands firmly at the top of the tree. The phenomenal success of Heather McKay as the world leader, in a class of her own, has become a by-word in Australia; so much so that one cosmetic company has full-page colour advertisements in the mass circulation weekly women's magazine showing Heather endorsing their products.

The widespread acceptance of the sport as a distinctive part of the nation's leisure fabric, and the hard-earned success from sound and enthusiastic administration has led to the continuation of the healthy, expanding, and thrusting squash scene in Australia.

NEW ZEALAND 1974

Brian Humberstone

The thirst of leading New Zealand squash players for tours overseas and visits from international teams must surely have been quenched in 1974. One wonders if such a bold policy can be maintained in these uncertain times. Looking back on 1974 makes one almost dizzy at the thought of so many squash players winging their way in and out of the country.

No fewer than 16 players with three officials were dispatched to the Australian championships in Adelaide in August, while this country played hosts to Australian women's, junior, and colts sides; a Great Britain men's team; and those old friends Geoff Hunt and Ken Hiscoe on a professional exhibition and tournament tour. Late in the year the association also sent two of their leading men, Trevor Colyer and Neven Barbour, on a 45-day tour of Britain.

Tours undeniably raise the standards of the top players. Perhaps a fine example is the visit of the Great Britain women's team to New Zealand in the 1960s, when they were far too good for the locals. But in the early 1970s, following much competition with Australia, New Zealand beat a strong British women's side in Auckland in an international, and then made a triumphant tour of Britain a year later.

The past season has revealed that there is another important factor governing the standard of the game. Leading players, especially men, simply cannot make a succession of tours, as was shown by the marked number of stars who were not available for the Australian tour. In fact none of the male players who played in the 1973 international series in South Africa were available for selection, most crying off because of work commitments.

The 1974 tours had their good and bad news. It was good news that the New Zealand men were able to beat a Great Britain side 2-1 in a Test series. But it was bad news that the Australian women should make a clean sweep of their international series in this country, and that the Australian colts should trounce a New Zealand team in one international without the loss of a match.

The season produced no prospective world beater from its many tournaments and tours, and the ranking lists for the year had very much of a stay-put look about them.

Neven Barbour retained his national men's title with a most impressive victory over the rising Queenslander Terry Cheetham, and after some years in the first two or three, Mrs Jenny Webster at last won her first New Zealand women's championship. The most significant advances made last year were by the young Rotorua player, Bruce Brownlee, and the former New Zealand Davis Cup team man, Howard Broun.

Brownlee is a determined young man, and has made a tour of Britain in a freelance capacity. He could be the one who will emerge as a player of real international quality.

Broun rose from nine to three in the rankings, giving some very good displays early in the season. But he was rather disappointing in the international series against Great Britain.

The Rothmans coaching scheme entered its fifth year, and has been responsible for producing some fine young juniors. But the big question is whether or not these juniors, after trips to Australia, will continue to advance and cut a swathe in the senior ranks.

The growth of the game continues in spectacular fashion. The national body now commands an affiliated membership of 29,772, as compared with 26,575 the previous year, and only 16,629 in 1967. Club memberships are being sorely tested as more and more people are banging at the doors seeking entry. If there is the money – and it can be shown to be a handsome investment – commercial centres appear to be the only way of introducing more players into the game.

Perhaps the most historic event of 1974 was the opening of the first glass-backed court in New Zealand at the North Shore club. Other clubs are following closely behind.

So all looks well for the game said to be the fastest growing sport in New Zealand; and administrators will be out to see that there is no easing off in the coming year.

NEW ZEALAND CHAMPIONSHIPS
Hamilton, 12–20 July

MEN'S CHAMPIONSHIP – SEMI-FINALS

N. S. Barbour (Henderson) bt H. A. Broun (Henderson)
1-9, 9-4, 9-0, 9-0

T. Cheetham (Australia) bt T. Johnston (Rotorua)
5-9, 9-5, 6-9, 9-7, 9-0

FINAL

Barbour bt Cheetham 9-4, 9-1, 9-2

WOMEN'S CHAMPIONSHIP – SEMI-FINALS

J. Webster (Manurewa bt C. Fleming (Eden Epsom)
9-3, 9-2, 5-9, 4-9, 9-4

P. Buckingham (Henderson) bt J. Lamb (Khandallah)
9-3, 9-4, 9-3

FINAL

Webster bt Buckingham 9-4, 9-3, 5-9, 9-2

INTERNATIONALS

AUSTRALIA v NEW ZEALAND (WOMEN)

FIRST TEST

Auckland, 26 May 1974

L. Hubinger (Australia) bt P. Buckingham (NZ)
8-10, 4-9, 9-1, 9-6, 9-3
C. Van Nierop (Australia) bt C. Fleming (NZ) 9-4, 9-6, 9-3
L. Chapman (Australia) lost to J. Webster (NZ) 4-9, 7-9, 9-3, 5-9
Australia won 2-1

SECOND TEST

Hamilton, 30 May 1974

L. Hubinger (Australia) bt P. Buckingham (NZ) 9-7, 9-0, 9-1
C. Van Nierop (Australia) bt J. Webster (NZ)
9-10, 9-2, 7-9, 9-4, 9-7
L. Chapman (Australia) lost to J. Lamb (NZ) 9-3, 5-9, 6-9, 6-9
Australia won 2-1

THIRD TEST

Wellington, 6 June 1974

L. Hubinger (Australia) bt J. Webster (NZ) 9-3, 0-9, 9-5, 9-4
A. Smith (Australia) bt P. Buckingham (NZ) 9-1, 9-5, 9-2
C. Van Nierop (Australia) bt J. Lamb (NZ) 9-4, 9-0, 9-5
Australia won 3-0

NEW ZEALAND v SRA (MEN)

FIRST TEST

Auckland, 29 May 1974

T. Johnston (NZ) lost to M. D. Thurgur (GB) 9-1, 5-9, 4-9, 4-9
H. A. Broun (NZ) lost to I. Robinson (GB) 1-9, 4-9, 2-9
N. S. Barbour (NZ) bt R. R. Chalmers (GB) 2-9, 9-6, 10-8,
4-9, 9-5
Great Britain won 2-1

SECOND TEST

Wellington, 6 June 1974

T. Johnston (NZ) bt M. D. Thurgur (GB) 9-1, 9-2, 9-1
H. A. Broun (NZ) lost to I. Robinson (GB) 4-9, 4-9, 9-3, 9-10
N. S. Barbour (NZ) bt R. R. Chalmers (GB) 9-3, 9-3, 2-9, 9-3
New Zealand won 2-1

THIRD TEST

Christchurch, 13 June 1974

T. Johnston (NZ) bt M. D. Thurgur (GB) 9-2, 9-5, 9-2
H. A. Broun (NZ) lost to I. Robinson (GB) 8-10, 5-9, 7-9
N. S. Barbour (NZ) bt R. R. Chalmers (GB) 7-9, 9-3, 9-7, 9-3
New Zealand won 2-1

Is this what squash is really *all about?*

JUST JONAH

Mike Palmer

Ask Jonah Barrington what he does besides playing squash and he'll list watching television, reading, and listening to music: but not necessarily in that order or with any particular depth of feeling. This is understandable – for anyone who has ever visited the Barrington household will wonder how anything that is not squash-shaped can ever claim part of his single-minded life. Even the Barrington dog, a beach mongrel adopted from Kenya's shores, came from an African squash tour; but Jonah did have the decency to insist that Nicholas Charles, the newly-arrived Barrington junior, could be excused court training for the first six months of his life.

If all this implies that Barrington has adopted a fanatical approach to his sport, then the player himself would be the last to deny it. However, Barrington talking about Barrington emerges as a paradoxical figure, still incurably fired by ambition, but with the drive now tempered by maturity.

He admits that, for the first time in his life, hitting a squash ball comes second to the family life for which he has longed but only recently begun to achieve or even enjoy. Barrington at 34, the family man, is a different proposition to the lonely figure who nine years ago first won a major title. A wife and child have given him the personal happiness and assurance that a thousand squash victories could never bring.

Gradually one realises that Barrington has missed out his second favourite pastime from his list – that of talking. He has an eloquence tinged with conviction which makes him more than just an interesting conversationalist. If he didn't talk he would paint; the words flow out in a tide of self-expression that if it found its way on to canvas would cause storage problems.

He talks lucidly and above all, honestly.

'Becoming a father was a vital part of my life. It was something worth waiting for and about which I became very excited. I think that it is much more important than hitting a squash ball, although there was a time when I would have contested the issue. Now, if it is a toss up between the family and squash, the family must win.

'But because squash is my job and not a serious hobby,

because it is our way of securing the future, I work at it as systematically as I can.

'I'm 34 and my trainer, Bomber Harris, thinks there is a lot to come. The schedule that I will be covering over the next two or three years will surprise a lot of people; the results too, I hope will be a surprise. I want to achieve what I achieved before and the incentive is that the standard is now that much higher, making a comeback that much harder, and therefore more personally satisfying if I win through.

'I want to stay in competitive squash but I've got to be an outstanding player and by that I mean one of the top three. I know I cannot be No. 1 all the time, yet there is such a thing as job satisfaction, even in squash.

'I have also got a responsibility, something which I felt very much during the last British Open, that of being the only British player in with a chance. Many people came up to me and said, "We're relying on you". I feel I have an obligation to continue because if I fall away I cannot see any other player being able to replace me and that's not being immodest. Most of the players around with talent are amateurs and likely to remain so. They can only go so far and it's a situation that is not likely to change in Britain for the next 10 years.'

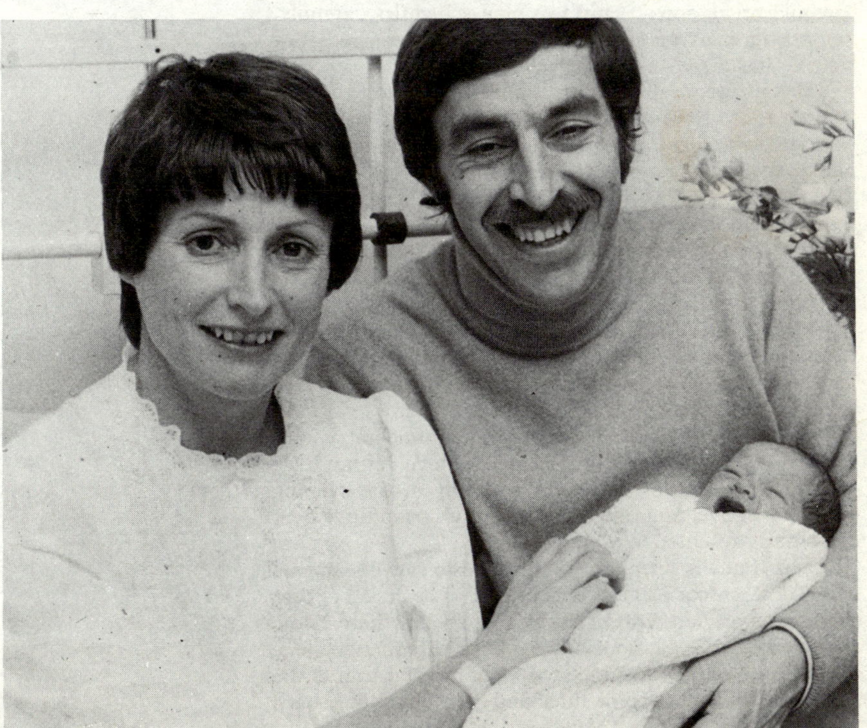

A world squash champion of the future? Nicholas Barrington, son of Madeleine and Jonah, will surely have all the coaching he needs. (Beaverbrook Newspapers)

Barrington feels that it is his responsibility to maintain himself over this period, although the intensity of approach he shows to training raises the question of how long he can go on. A feeling that he has 'so much more to give' perhaps clouds his judgement on the amount of physical punishment his body can take, although it would be totally wrong to underestimate him in this respect.

He admits: 'There is an immense amount of physical discomfort in the training work I do' – a statement that at face value is a glib dismissal of the limits to which Barrington has pushed himself. For discomfort, read pain.

'When I began 10 years ago I punished myself viciously, a startling reaction to what had gone before. In fact I trained so hard there was a period when I had nightmares about what I had to do the next day.

'I don't have them now because my body and mind have been conditioned to accepting a lot of pressure and I'm better organised in what I do. I know that in the past I have done a lot of training during which I broke myself down instead of achieving a build up.

'An old friend of mine in Australia, Aub Amos, who runs a squash centre in Brisbane told me "you need to abuse the body to toughen it". I have benefited from this approach but I could not do that programme now because I would break down. I have to plan schedules carefully.'

Barrington's training now has to take into consideration that he has a son.

'This means that I get up very early and go for a run.

'I do up to seven miles, come home, have a sleep and then go on to a court around mid-morning where I hit a ball on my own for an hour. Then I have a break and start again around 5.30pm hopefully with a practice game with an opponent of good standard but that depends on who is around. Then there is the training with Bomber, so the greater part of my day is spent around training or preparing to train.

'When I am at home, Madeleine and I watch a lot of television together. We find that very relaxing and we also like to read a lot. Spy thrillers by John Le Carré or Len Deighton are very easy on the mind.

'A social life? Because I spend so much time away from home, I just enjoy being in the house. I love getting back after a tour. Any interruptions, certainly in the evening when we are settling down and the day's training is over are bitterly resented.

'I feel that the telephone is an intrusion or if someone comes to the door I find it difficult not to be rude because this is our private world. The people around here know that we like to be left alone and we have infrequent callers. I like to get settled into a period at home and that is the time when I feel I become fitter and mentally more sharp than at any other time.'

It is this domestic and personal stability on which Barrington can now rely that has helped him to recover from the loss of his British Open title and find the determination to remould his approach to squash. A comparison between Barrington's loss and that suffered by Geoff Hunt at Wembley in February 1975 is impossible but Barrington makes a telling assessment of the problems that now face the Australian.

'He is not as badly placed as I was when I lost my title. Mine went in disastrous circumstances. Geoff's basic assets are greater than mine and there's no doubt that he has more potential. Whether he develops this potential is up to him, what system he uses to bring it out we'll have to see, but the message should be clear to him. If he continues playing on the same lines he's not going to have the same success. It's a law of diminishing returns.

'I expected Zaman to have a reaction after his Open victory and that Hunt would tear into him. A couple of occasions after I had beaten Hunt he made me suffer for it but he couldn't shake Zaman so we must judge the Pakistani's performances as even better than they appear. For me he is No. 1 for 1975.'

Barrington is equally realistic about his own prospects, even visualising a time ahead when his own career will be over. He doesn't dwell long on these thoughts and his tone becomes almost wistful when he says:

'I try and detach myself sometimes and think from the point of view of Barrington not taking part and things going on without him and how he will react.

'I hope that the decision to stop playing will come while I am still hale and hearty. I hope that injury doesn't stop me, and that I will finish because I have realised that I cannot sustain myself at a high level and that it is the logical thing to do.

'I think I will always be connected with the sport. I won't become secretary of the SRA but I would like to see players well looked after, well organised.

'I would also like to be involved with individuals who are fanatically keen about the sport; probably at some stage with a group that wants to get to the top and will be able to undertake the sort of programme the Pakistanis have done over the last few years.

'That would really please me, yet . . . I am always restless and my ambitions can never be diluted.'

DEVELOPMENT OF THE PROFESSIONAL GAME

Robert Jolly

Traditionally a professional squash player lurked in squash courts, putting club members through their paces in a day divided into endless half-hourly sessions – day in, day out – until a late retirement, whence he turned to refereeing, committee-sitting, or administration.

The size of the prize-money that has accompanied the major championships in recent years has changed a generation of amateurs and shamateurs into fully fledged touring professionals. Some still have to learn their craft completely, while some find only moderate recompense for the hard graft; but above all they have clearly declared their status and the label 'professional squash player' no longer relates simply to the club coach. Indeed, images are beginning to be projected, and the flavour of glamorous jet-setting to international tournaments is being stirred into the professional hot-pot.

In 1974 most of the leading pros grouped together under the banner now entitled the International Squash Professionals Association. Player power has arrived. ISPA has several functions on offer to the squash world in return for the continual pressing for higher, and better-regulated, rewards from tournament play.

The prize-money distribution methods between players, the setting of minimum expense allowances, the payment of travel expenses (especially for international journeys), guarantees, and appearance money, are all financial subjects for which ISPA has set guidelines to be considered by national associations and tournament organisers. But ISPA is as yet too young to have established a rock-hard power base, and relationships with national and international amateur and professional governing bodies have still to be cemented. The subject of a World Open Championship, however is likely to draw the various organisations together, with ISPA at the hub as the representative body of the integral ingredients, the players.

Last year a private promoter staged an international invitation event in Melbourne, Australia, calling itself *a* World Open event, much to the displeasure of the International Squash Rackets Federation – the supreme authority in world squash.

The sport lacks an ultimate tournament of world stature,

and will continue to make do with the British Open as a *de facto* world title. An officially sanctioned event has been the aspiration of many entrepreneurs as well as the ISRF. The Federation's current notion is to rename in alternate years the Australian and British Open competitions as the World Open Championships. This woolly proposal has been further complicated by a request from Pakistan to hold a World Open in Karachi. Naturally, every squash-playing nation would care for a piece of the action.

The related issue of amateur status being forsaken for completely open squash, so fiercely rejected by Australian officialdom, is finally swinging towards the British way of thinking: considering all competitors as simply players, without the difficult distinction between amateurs and professionals. International Test matches would then be expected to follow the lead of the PIA (Pakistan International Airways), who sponsored the Great Britain versus Pakistan clash at Wembley in January, 1975 – the first open national team event ever held. The opportunity for the professionals to represent their countries once again would appeal to players and followers alike.

Within this spectrum, sponsorship grows apace throughout the world, creating new earning opportunities each season. A comprehensive circuit is being welded across the vast expanse of Australia, whilst in South Africa the already successful bout of tournaments staged by Owen Emslie was augmented in 1974 for the first time with a national open championship.

Prize-money and expenses are attractively high in southern Africa. They can only be bettered in Europe by two events – the British Open Championship sponsored by Benson and Hedges for the three years up to 1975, and the inaugural British Caledonian-Yellow Dot Grand Prix. The latter offered total prize-money of £12,475 spread between eight professionals, with the winner capable of earning £3,500 in only 15 matches.

Most of the sponsorship cash derives from companies outside the squash business. Economic pressures in the western world have certainly affected the growth of squash sponsorship, but have not checked its progress drastically. Professional promotion and the growing acceptance throughout the media mean that squash commands ever increasing attention as an alternative to the sports traditionally considered to be promotional vehicles.

The earning power of the professional is running at an all-time high. However, exhibition fees have outstripped the income factor on galleried courts specifically designed in the 1970s to make exhibition work pay off, not only for the players but for the owners as well. There is a general imbalance between the income expected by the top pros and the current capacity of the British public to pay.

This is a temporary situation, a symptom of the room for

Jonah Barrington, chairman of the International Squash Players Association, symbolises the emergence of 'player power' in the game. He has outspoken views on the rewards that professionals should receive from tournament play.

adjustment in this rapidly developing sector of squash. The establishment of television coverage may well be the financial panacea at this stage.

As the marketing of products expands in proportion to the increase in squash popularity at all levels, so too does equipment endorsement for professionals. The names of the leading players adorn rackets, clothing, shoes, energising soft drinks, even squash court construction processes. The next step, as players gain a wider following, is for the stars to lend their autographs to products indirectly related to squash, products which are consumed by a market into which the average squash player falls.

Club affiliation, as in the world of golf, will also be new ground for squash professionals to exploit. By making a certain number of personal appearances each year, and associating a prestigious name with the club, the notion of a club professional will have turned full circle in the working relationship between the professional squash player and the club.

However, there is, and will continue to be, a place for the sound instructor of squash – however far-removed the top flight of tournament players becomes as a result of ever-increasing prize-money.

MAJOR BRITISH AMATEUR TOURNAMENTS 1974-75

BRITISH AMATEUR CHAMPIONSHIP 1974

The 1974 British Amateur Championship, held at Wembley for the first time, was again dominated by Pakistan but the performances of British players Philip Ayton and Peter Verow, who reached the semi-finals, sustained home interest in the tournament. Each was making his first appearance at that stage of the competition; and for Ayton the accomplishment was particularly sweet because he had already made six quarter-final appearances.

Predictably, both were beaten – Ayton by the defending and eventual champion, Mohibullah Khan, and Verow by the mercurial Qamar Zaman. This resulted in a repeat of the previous year's final, which was not suprising since the two young Pakistanis were clearly several classes ahead of their nearest challengers.

If Mohibullah's crown was to have been threatened, then the likely source, apart from Zaman, was another Pakistani, Sajjad Muneer. Muneer was seeded third, but failed to appear; this gave an unbalanced look to the draw, in which three South Africans, Selwyn Machet (No. 6), Doug Barrow (No. 7), and Dave Scott (No. 8), ranked surprisingly high.

In the other half of the draw, Ray Lewis of Australia, who could have expected to make considerable headway, did not turn up either. The absence of these players took a lot of bite from the competition.

The first round merely confirmed the awesome talents of Mohibullah and Zaman, the former dropping just five points and Zaman only one in·their opening matches. Zaman's inventiveness and incredible range of shots make him one of the most delightful players to watch and many people felt that his talent was capable of lifting the title.

Two of the South Africans, Dave Scott and Selwyn Machet, struggled to move beyond the first round, although it must be pointed out that Machet nursed an ankle injury during the whole of his stay in the tournament. However, his unusual style of pace and stroke eventually accounted for Alan Purnell, the Worcester champion, while Barrow was extended to five games by the persistent and enthusiastic Mike Westrup of Kent.

The bright spots for Britain were a welcome return to form by international Paul Millman, and the win by Peter Verow over a younger member of the Pakistani team, Atlas Khan.

Millman, facing the fourth ranked Pakistani, Abdul Rahman, produced a length of drive and flurry of drop shots which won him the opening two games. He then seemed to lose his concentration in the third and Rahman was allowed to escape a match ball and keep alive. The loss of the game had the desired effect on Millman, who, although never running away with the fourth, showed enough aggression to win it 9–7.

Kevin Shawcross carried the burden of being the only Australian in the draw, but at 6 feet 3 inches and 14½ stone he was well capable of doing so. For a big man he is deceptively fast around the court, as South African Scott found to his cost in the second round. The match went to five games before Shawcross emerged triumphant to cause the first seeding upset.

If this was a minor shock, then the departure of Springbok Doug Barrow should have caused a national celebration in Sweden. He also lost in five, to young Swede Michael Hellstrom. The match contained plenty of drama, with Hellstrom fighting back from two games down with his penetrating shots, as Barrow's length began to falter. It was good to see a player from an emergent squash nation performing so well, and Hellstrom's achievement is significant of the advances being made in that country.

All Britain's hopefuls moved successfully into the third round; Ayton at the expense of Mike Nathanson, the Swedish-based South African, Mike Corby in four games over Hugh Colburn, Peter Verow against wiry Scot Kim Bruce-Lockhart, and Millman over the up-and-coming Ian Robinson. The latter's performance was disappointing: the Yorkshire champion looked as though he was suffering from the effects of too much squash.

And so into the third round, the first real 'crunch' stage of the competition. One notable British loss was unavoidable with Ayton and Corby drawn against each other, and although the pair have fought some very close duels, Ayton was the victor by a wide margin on this occasion.

Millman and another Briton, Pat Kirton, departed – courtesy of Mohibullah and Zaman – while John Richardson will still be cursing himself for the match balls he wasted in the fourth game against Mohammed Saleem. Richardson had another chance when he was ahead in the fifth, but again failed to use his advantage, with disastrous results.

The game emphasised the tenacious qualities of Saleem, whose style lacks all the usual rhythm one might associate with a player of his standing. He can often be found in losing positions but has the ability to summon reserves of skill and resilience which his opponents find most disconcerting.

Machet and Verow marched on, but for giant-killer Hellstrom it was the end. The Swede fell to the experience of New Zealand's Trevor Collyer but could go home still feeling really proud of his efforts.

Shawcross emerged victorious from a tremendous match with Egyptian Gamal Awad, who was a losing qualifier but entered the draw because former amateur champion Aftab Jawaid did not arrive. This time Awad found himself stretched beyond his limits.

Ayton's destruction of Saleem to enter the semi-finals was possibly one of the most entertaining matches of the Championship. Both served up a delightful variety of angled and drop shots with a delicacy of touch that brought murmurs of approval from an intrigued audience. Saleem attacked relentlessly, yet could not daunt the adventurous spirit and fine execution of Ayton, who won in straight games.

Less impressive was the performance of Verow in beating Machet. It was a scrappy affair with play rarely reaching championship standard; Verow should have sewn it up without letting the South African drag him to five games.

Mohibullah trounced Shawcross 3–0. Both men struck the ball powerfully but the telling factor was the Pakistani's accuracy. Zaman did not waste too much time in joining his countryman, although Collyer did not give in without some brisk resistance during their three games.

Ayton began his semi-final against Mohibullah in the best possible way, winning the first game 10–9 as the Pakistani was forced into what, for him, were some unusual errors. The accuracy and pace of Ayton's attack had clearly surprised the defending champion, but this effort was to take its toll of the British player.

Mohibullah came out for the second game determined to put pressure on Ayton; this he did by taking the ball very early. The struggle lasted until 3–3, when Mohibullah began to win points in an ominous fashion. Now it was a question of Ayton trying to regain the initiative – but his reserves were gone. He disputed the third game with some spirit and then collapsed in the fourth without winning another point.

The manner of Zaman's win over Verow was even more emphatic with Verow baffled by the Pakistani's prodigious shot-making. It was a straight-games win for Zaman, thus bringing about the final clash the seeding committee had predicted.

The final did not produce the thrills of the previous year. Mohibullah set the pattern with his ruthless hounding of the ball, driving his opponent to the back of the court and forcing him to go for his shots in unfavourable positions. Under this pressure Zaman frequently hit down after the frustration of long and exhausting rallies.

Mohibullah's safety-first tactics made it an unimpressive match in terms of entertainment. The one period when his domination was threatened was when he lost the third game after incurring several penalty points. It was a situation that could have disturbed some players, but Mohibullah showed a maturity and discipline beyond his years. Coolly he reasserted himself to win the Championship for the second year running.

RESULTS

FIRST ROUND

Mohibullah Khan (Pak) bt R. Yorke-Long (Eng) 9-2, 9-1, 9-2
M. Awad (Egypt) bt G. Collins (SA) 9-1, 9-3, 9-4
P. Kirton (Eng) bt A. Colburn (SA) 9-5, 9-7, 5-9, 9-3
C. Stahl (Eng) bt M. Mitha (Uganda) 9-3, 9-4, 9-6
D. Scott (SA) bt M. Westrup (Eng) 6-9, 9-2, 9-3, 7-9, 9-6
K. Shawcross (Aus) bt J. Beattie (Wales) 9-2, 7-9, 9-2, 9-2
G. Awad (Egypt) bt P. Cattrall (Eng) 9-5, 9-6, 9-1
K. Dowling (SA) bt R. Johnson (Eng) 9-2, 3-9, 9-5, 9-1
P. Ayton (Eng) bt T. Wheeler 9-0, 9-2, 9-1
M. Nathanson (Swe) bt R. Shay (Rho) 9-3, 6-9, 9-3, 9-5
H. Colburn (Eng) bt J. McGrath (Ire) 9-3, 10-8, 5-9, 9-2
M. Corby (Eng) bt A. Waddy (Eng) 9-7, 5-9, 9-0, 9-4
M. Saleem (Pak) bt N. Martin (Scot) 9-5, 9-3, 9-5
W. Sabey (Eng) bt J. Leslie (Eng) 9-5, 4-9, 9-5, 9-7
H. Higazy (Egypt) bt M. Peasley (Eng) 9-3, 9-7, 9-3
J. Richardson (Eng) bt I. Holding (SA) 9-3, 9-7, 9-4
S. Aly (Egypt) bt J. Le Lievre (Guer) 9-3, 9-0, 9-0
Maqsood Ahmed (Pak) bt P. Chard (Papua) 9-4, 9-1, 9-3
P.White (Eng) bt F. af Ekenstam (Swe) 4-9, 9-7, 9-3, 9-2
S. Machet (SA) bt A. Purnell (Worcs) 9-7, 9-7, 0-9, 10-8
N. Barbour (NZ) bt P. Kenyon (Eng) 9-2, 10-8, 9-1
P. Verow (Eng) bt Atlas Khan (Pak) 5-9, 9-4, 9-5, 9-1
K. Bruce-Lockhart (Scot) bt C. Zweigbergk (Eng) 9-0, 2-9, 9-2, 9-1
R. Chalmers (Scot) bt H. Salo (Fin) 9-3, 9-0, 9-2
M. Helal (Egypt) bt J. Sier (Can) 9-4, 9-1, 9-5
T. Collyer (NZ) bt I. Dowdeswell (Rho) 9-4, 5-9, 2-9, 9-4, 9-5
M. Hellstrom (Swe) bt R. O'Connor (SA) 9-5, 9-3, 9-6
D. Barrow (SA) bt J. Stockenburg (Swe) 9-3, 9-1, 9-3
I. Robinson (Eng) bt B. Brownlee (NZ) 9-3, 9-4, 9-3
P. Millman (Eng) bt Abdul Rahman (Pak) 9-5, 9-1, 9-10, 9-7
A. Aklouba (Egypt) bt H. Bucht (Fin) 9-1, 9-0, 9-0
Q. Zaman (Pak) bt C. Orriss (Eng) 9-1, 9-0, 9-0

SECOND ROUND

M. Khan bt Awad 9-3, 9-3, 9-5
Kirton bt Stahl 9-7, 5-9, 9-6, 9-0
Shawcross bt Scott 6-9, 9-2, 9-5, 9-10, 10-8
Awad bt Dowling 9-7, 8-10, 3-9, 9-0, 9-3
Ayton bt Nathanson 9-4, 9-0, 9-0
Corby bt Colburn 4-9, 9-7, 9-6, 9-0

Saleem bt Sabey 10-8, 9-5, 9-6
Richardson bt Higazy 10-8, 9-2, 8-10, 9-0
Aly bt Maqsood 9-0, 10-8, 9-5
Machet bt White 9-4, 9-4, 9-5
Verow bt Barbour 9-2, 9-4, 4-9, 9-4
Bruce-Lockhart bt Chalmers 9-4, 5-9, 10-8, 3-9, 9-2
Collyer bt Helal 9-7, 6-9, 1-9, 9-4, 9-4
Hellstrom bt Barrow 5-9, 6-9, 9-3, 9-2, 9-5
Millman bt Robinson 9-5, 9-5, 9-6
Zaman bt Allouba 9-2, 9-2, 9-2

THIRD ROUND
Khan bt Mirton 9-0, 9-0, 9-1
Shawcross bt Awad 9-2, 10-8, 9-7
Ayton bt Corby 9-5, 9-1, 9-4
Saleem bt Richardson 9-2, 6-9, 9-6, 8-10, 9-7
Machet bt Aly 9-7, 9-6, 9-5
Verow bt Bruce-Lockhart 9-3, 9-1, 6-9, 9-5
Collyer bt Hellstrom 9-0, 9-5, 1-9, 9-5
Zaman bt Millman 9-1, 9-2, 9-0

FOURTH ROUND
Khan bt Shawcross 9-6, 9-1, 9-5
Ayton bt Saleem 9-3, 9-5, 9-7
Verow bt Machet 9-5, 2-9, 9-2, 9-10, 9-1
Zaman bt Collyer 9-3, 10-8, 9-0

SEMI-FINALS
Khan bt Ayton 9-10, 9-3, 9-6, 9-0
Zaman bt Verow 9-1, 9-5, 9-5

FINAL
Khan bt Zaman 10-8, 9-5, 5-9, 9-5

BRITISH ABBEYDALE INVITATION TOURNAMENT

'If it is run by Abbeydale it must be good.' This consensus of opinion is generally held in the squash world. The slogan may sound corny, even trite, but the message is true.

While the move of the British Open to the new complex at Wembley was accepted, there was more than a tinge of sadness that the 'Abbeydale treatment' would be missing. Wembley's concrete corridors cannot yet compete with the atmosphere and spirit that seems to be part of the fabric of the Sheffield club. Possibly it was the knowledge that they would not be running the 1975 Open that made Abbeydale try even harder with their own tournament, an invitation event with many of Britain's leading amateurs competing.

The tournament was first held in 1969, one of the first weekend competitions which welcomed local and national players and gave local audiences the chance of seeing first-class match play. Sponsorship was introduced in 1972 and for the 1974 tournament, Thorntons, the Sheffield-based but nationally known confectionery manufacturer, stepped in as backers. Their contribution helped produce a magnificent four days of squash, including a final that will long be remembered.

Mike Corby will remember it more than most, not because he reached the final, but because he let Philip Ayton off the hook and robbed himself of a victory that would have been the climax to a fine comeback to senior squash.

Corby, man of many talents, and a British hockey international, three times had Ayton within a point of defeat. In the minds of the spectators it seemed inconceivable that Corby could lose. He seemed so much in control and a desperately tired Ayton was just hanging on.

It says much for Ayton's resolve and stamina that he eventually won the 95-minute battle. He took the first two games comfortably with greater control and accuracy but tired visibly in the third and fourth when Corby began to take the ball very early. In the fifth game Corby led 8-5 and 8-6, only to see the advantage disappear. Ayton's persistence and determination to keep the ball in play paid off as he levelled at 8-8. The effect on Corby was shattering. His position of dominance had gone and Ayton stayed in hand to win 9-5, 9-7, 4-9, 3-9, 10-8.

Philip Ayton defended his No. 1 ranking with great skill and resolve, none more so than during the final of the Abbeydale Invitation event. He is seen here representing Britain in the Test Series against Pakistan.

RESULTS

FIRST ROUND

P. Ayton bt P. Kenyon 9-4, 9-3, 9-3
J. Leslie bt P. Kirton 2-9, 9-5, 9-4, 9-3
J. Richardson bt J. Kingston 9-3, 9-6, 9-1
N. Martin bt I. Nuttall 3-9, 2-9, 10-8, 9-3, 9-3
K. Bruce-Lockhart bt I. Robinson 9-7, 9-3, 9-3
M. Corby bt R. Chalmers 9-6, 7-9, 9-1, 9-6
P. Millman bt N. Stewart 9-4, 9-4, 9-2
P. Verow bt W. Sabey 7-9, 9-1, 9-5, 9-0

SECOND ROUND

Ayton bt Leslie 9-4, 9-1, 9-2
Richardson bt Martin 9-2, 10-8, 9-4
Corby bt Bruce-Lockhart 1-9, 5-9, 9-5, 9-3, 9-6
Verow bt Millman 9-3, 9-4, 9-4

SEMI-FINALS

Ayton bt Richardson 9-4, 2-9, 9-4, 9-0
Corby bt Verow 10-8, 9-6, 9-0

FINAL

Ayton bt Corby 9-5, 9-7, 4-9, 3-9, 10-8

ROLEX BRITISH CLOSED

British amateur squash produced its first official champion when 24-year-old barrister Jonathan Leslie won the Rolex British Closed at Wembley in March 1975. His victory was a fascinating climax to a remarkable tournament, an event hit by mishap and injury but providing a form of competition that has been missing from the calendar.

Philip Ayton, No. 1 seed, withdrew with 'flu on the opening day, Peter Verow, No. 3, scratched after a training injury on the third day, and fourth seed John Richardson went home ill after losing an exciting semi-final. In addition, Mike Corby, the official second favourite, played throughout with a heavy cold and had considered pulling out.

It says much for the event that these problems were overcome, while the eventual result pushed to the front a player who might otherwise have stayed in the background for another season or two.

The format – a round robin for 16 players with eight direct entry and eight qualifiers – was tough, but it was generally accepted afterwards as having been fair and stimulating. Promising youngsters such as Yorkshire's Brian Pearson, with no pretensions to eventual victory, gained invaluable experience through having three matches in their group against more senior players.

Jonathan Leslie (left) was the shock winner of the Rolex British Amateur Closed. His final with Stuart Courtney (right) provided a fitting climax to the new tournament. (Photo by Joseph Singer)

Stuart Courtney was able to launch his comeback into top squash against a background of testing competition. His re-emergence after several months of wrestling with business problems gave added quality to the entry, and posed a real threat to the seeding. It was no surprise that he reached the final, dealing ruthlessly with a groggy Mike Corby in the semis, although it was always likely that anyone able to engage him in an attritional match would prove his fitness suspect.

Leslie was able to do this, conceding the first two games and then gradually wearing his opponent down until the end result became a formality.

When Leslie stepped forward to take the Rolex trophy, he could hardly have imagined that he would have reached the semi-finals, let alone win the tournament – but he had taken his opportunity well. Two weeks later he was given his first England cap to conclude, for him, a memorable season.

John Richardson played consistently well throughout the British season and deservedly moved to No. – in the rankings.

GROUPINGS

Group A J. Richardson, K. Bruce-Lockhart, B. Pearson, C. Bridge
Winner – Richardson.

Group B M. Corby, P. Kirton, R. Carter, A. Purnell
Winner – Corby.

Group C P. Verow, J. Leslie, P. Kenyon, R. Johnson
Winner – Leslie.

Group D N. Stewart, I. Robinson, S. Courtney, A. Lusty
Winner – Courtney.

Semi-finals Leslie bt Richardson 3-9, 9-3, 9-7, 6-9, 9-6
Courtney bt Corby 9-3, 9-4, 3-9, 9-0

Final Leslie bt Courtney 6-9, 8-10, 9-3, 9-3, 9-2

LANGHAM LIFE HOME INTERNATIONALS

17–19 January, Newport
Scotland 4 Wales 1 Scotland 2 Ireland 3
Scotland 0 England 5 Ireland 0 England 5
Ireland 4 Wales 1 England 5 Wales 0

Team standing
1 England, 2 Ireland, 3 Scotland, 4 Wales
TEAMS
England: (P. Ayton, J. Richardson, P. Verow, P. Millman, I. Nuttall, M. Corby)
Ireland: (J. McGrath, R. Weir, B. Cranwell, G. Doherty, D. Byrne)
Scotland: (K. Bruce-Lockhart, R. Chalmers, N. Martin, N. Stewart, A. Minty, J. Done)
Wales: (R. Dolman, J. Beattie, I. Carlisle, C. Morgan, P. Wilson)

BANBURY TROPHY

19 April, Wembley
Brighton bt Abbeydale 3-2

THE AUSTRALIAN ANGLE

Geoff Hunt

Whenever people want to find an easy answer to the question 'Why are Australian sportsmen and women among the best in the world?' they generally point to the good climate which encourages year-round participation. That hardly holds good for the indoor game of squash; except it could be argued that plenty of sunshine in itself promotes better health, and that that is the reason why Australian players are fitter than most.

The weather could well be a contributory factor, but in finding the real reason I want at the same time to knock down the notion that Australian squash is some kind of true-blue reactionary force within the game, against change and against professionalism.

In Australia, squash is a game for the people. It covers a far greater range of social groupings than is the case in Britain – and it has been so for a long time. The sport's widespread appeal has produced vast numbers of players within a framework of intensive competition and it is *this* that has pushed Australia to the forefront of world squash.

Initially, in Australia as in Britain, most squash courts were in clubs. Perhaps the club's main function was tennis, bowling, or just social, but against this background squash took hold. The real impetus came in the middle 1950s with what we call commercial courts, the product of private enterprise.

Courts were not operated on a club basis. Anyone could come along and it was pay as you play. Permanent bookings were available for set periods, over say three months, and I think this works far better than the club system. At least you know when you can play and you do not have the trouble of having to book days in advance.

The Wembley Centre in London is the first squash centre in Britain to offer this kind of facility on a large scale, and its popularity shows why the Australian system has been such a success. Commercial court building continues to go ahead in Australia, with the club-type complex still very much in the minority.

As I see it, the advantage of the commercial centre is that someone with a couple of dollars in his pocket can feel like a game, play, and then, possibly, not play again for another six months. The beauty is that if he has the money there is nothing to stop him playing. This kind of freedom has given squash its popularity in Australia and I think Britain has a long way to go in this respect.

This brings me to my main point; that in Australia there is the greatest chance of discovering good players from the competions that are played every week. I know there is plenty of county and local league squash in Britain; but I doubt if it matches the rivalry, or standard, of, say, the pennant competition in Melbourne, where the grades go down a long way. Teams meet every week, and our associations have done a tremendous job with the administration.

Players like Ken Hiscoe have emerged from this background and fortunately there have been a few to follow him. Each started with the right basic techniques, then by playing together they learnt a great deal more about the game and helped each other too.

At that time we trained harder and played harder thar any of our contemporaries in Britain, until Jonah Barrington came along and tipped the balance by doing more training than we did. He showed that he had enough talent and was prepared to work to exploit it. This type of approach was new because squash, like a lot of other

Geoff Hunt has played a leading part in establishing Australia as one of the dominant squash nations.

amateur sports, was enjoyed by people who played a couple of times a week. Suddenly, Australian players were playing every day. They still had their jobs, of course, but they were amateurs and the Australian Association has, all along, tried to maintain the difference between the two classes of players.

Professionals were small in number. But there was a demand for more coaches and in my own state, Victoria, we tried to persuade players to turn professional by allowing them to play in the weekly leagues – which is another way of saying that they were 'open leagues'.

I think Australia could justify claiming to be the first country to move into open squash and perhaps this fact may alter a few opinions about attitudes there.

The professional coach could not play in amateur tournaments, or for Australia, but these were the sacrifices he had to make. Britain has amateur coaches, a system with which I cannot agree. It breaks the rules on professionalism by allowing an amateur to coach while still being able to enjoy the advantages of the amateur player.

The Australian Association wants to keep amateur squash and it is easy to understand why. Australia has won the 1967, 1969, 1971, and 1973 world championships and is proud of this record. More than 95 per cent of squash in Australia is amateur and professionals are very much in the minority.

There is no active campaigning against professionals by the Association, nor any real depth of anti-professional feeling – but there isn't any help for them either. The Association is very happy to let the two classes of player exist side by side, as they do so well in golf.

What has happened is that a few countries, Britain included, have allowed players to exceed their amateur status – condoned sham-amateurism if you like. This is leading to the breakdown of the two codes; and the reason why eventually there will have to be open squash. When this happens, and whether it is within the next couple of years, depends very much upon the International Squash Rackets Federation and its attitude. I'm not too sure how well this body is functioning or how effectively they can reflect world opinion within the game; but the Federation *is* the world body, and a decision as important as going 'open' is something only Federation members can decide.

Australia, New Zealand, and South Africa are the countries seeking to maintain the distinctions, but I fear they are fighting the inevitable. From my point of view, open squash will militate against my interests as a professional because it will mean more people around who can earn money from the game.

My own feeling is that if there had been strict control, the dual system of amateur and professional would have worked . . . and worked well.

EUROPEAN TEAM CHAMPIONSHIP 1975

Forget the fact that England retained the Pilkington European team championship in Dublin in March 1975; the win was irrelevant in terms of the development of the European game.

Think instead about the growing and measured challenge from countries such as Sweden and Finland. Think about the brave, but hopeless, challenge of France competing for the first time. Think about the swelling ranks of the European Federation, now with a membership of 17 nations and the promise of more to come. These were the factors that made 1975 a significant year for Europe.

From now on, Wales, Scotland, and Ireland will not be able to look forward to a secure place in the top four. Sweden, with their victories over Wales and Ireland, have made sure of that; while Finland are striving hard to match the standards of their Scandinavian neighbours. This shift of power has, more than anything else, made the European event more acceptable than it has been in the past. Such a statement is in no way meant to malign what has gone before, but to emphasise the fact that when all four home countries, including England, can eventually feel threatened, then European squash will have come of age.

The playing side is progressing . . . but what of the other aspects? The Irish SRA made a masterful job of the championship organisation, setting standards that will be difficult to match. Pilkington can justly be termed brave pioneers with their sponsorship. Their generous support has given the event stature at a time when there would be few other companies willing to risk their money in such a way. They have another year to complete and the Federation must hope that, economic factors apart, Pilkington will feel that the effort has been rewarding and worthwhile.

At their annual meeting in Dublin the Federation talked buoyantly about expanding membership, of creating an individual championship, and even of a club event. The competition ideas would seem a little ahead of their time, but at least the outlook is positive: let us hope that it stays that way.

RESULTS

Wales 5 Netherlands 0
Sweden 5 Belgium 0
England 5 France 0
Scotland 5 Switzerland 0
Ireland 5 Denmark 0
Finland 5 Germany 0
England 5 Sweden 0
Belgium 3 Netherlands 2
Wales 5 France 0
Ireland 5 Finland 0
Switzerland 3 Germany 2
Denmark 0 Scotland 5
Netherlands 0 Sweden 5
Belgium 3 France 2
Wales 0 England 5
Denmark 0 Finland 5
Ireland 5 Switzerland 0
Scotland 5 Germany 0
Netherlands 0 England 5
Sweden 5 France 0
Belgium 0 Wales 5
Denmark 5 Switzerland 0
Germany 0 Ireland 5
Scotland 4 Finland 1
Belgium 0 England 5
Sweden 3 Wales 2
France 0 Netherlands 5
Denmark 4 Germany 1
Finland 5 Switzerland 0
Scotland 5 Ireland 0

FINAL

England 5 Scotland 0

THIRD-PLACE PLAY-OFF

Ireland 2 Sweden 3

PLAY-OFFS

Wales 4 Finland 1,
Belgium 0 Denmark 5
Netherlands 5 Switzerland 0
France 2 Germany 3

Final positions 1 England; 2 Scotland; 3 Sweden; 4 Ireland; 5 Wales; 6 Finland; 7 Denmark; 8 Belgium; 9 Netherlands; 10 Switzerland; 11 Germany; 12 France

GREAT BRITAIN v PAKISTAN

Open International

When the idea of an open international was first discussed in the autumn of 1974 it seemed that it would be an initiative that would die through the lack of a sponsor. The professionals were not likely to play without adequate fees or expenses, but amid the economic gloom the promise of commercial support was not good.

Then two refreshing things happened. First, Jonah Barrington set an example by saying that he would be prepared to play for nothing, thereby reviving the fond thought that the honour of representing one's country is still far from dead. Secondly, Pakistan International Airlines came forward to sponsor the event – the first open international where the best players of both countries could compete against each other.

Barrington's comments at the time are worth repeating. The man who last captained Britain as an amateur in 1969 said: 'Outside individual competition the highest honour a player can win is to be picked by his country. I am quite happy to play without a fee and am sure any professional would feel the same way. I don't feel at all embittered that I have been excluded for the past five years because of being a professional. This is because we at last have an opportunity to play together regardless of status.'

Barrington saw the international as the first positive step towards abolishing the distinction between amateurs and professionals and creating just 'players' – a cause he fervently believes in. 'I didn't think we would get the current situation', he said, 'but we must now think ahead in terms of a world team championship on an open basis.'

The wider implications of the international, from Britain's point of view at any rate, are more memorable than the match result because Pakistan again showed the dominance they had enjoyed during the amateur Test series. Nothing other than a victory for Pakistan was expected, but the inclusion of Barrington and Easter in the British side did give rise to the hope that a complete whitewash would be avoided.

Barrington came into the match fresh from victory over his old adversary Geoff Hunt, yet seemed to be suffering from reaction. Gogi Alauddin's speed and fitness overwhelmed Barrington in the first two games, and indeed

Mike Corby's return at the age of 34 added much life to the British amateur scene. His explosive personality and all-court artistry make him a welcome addition to British international teams.

Mohibullah Khan's second successive victory in the British Amateur was somewhat overshadowed by the performances of his colleague, Zaman, later in the season.

the British player suffered the embarrassment of collecting only one of the first 14 points. Alauddin played with great assurance, delighting the spectators with his ability to hit a backhand cross-court shot into the nick, seemingly whenever he felt the need.

Over-confidence on Alauddin's part then allowed Barrington to find something of a rhythm so that the match took on a more balanced appearance, as Barrington took the third game 10-8. The Pakistani heeded the warning; for although Jonah continued to fight hard, Gogi reasserted himself.

Philip Ayton, nowhere near as sharp as he can be, was no match for the speedy Qamar Zaman, and John Richardson was beaten in four by Sajjad Muneer. This gave Pakistan a winning 3-0 lead, and the programme was duly completed by Mohibullah Khan and Mohammed Yasin accounting for John Easter and Mike Corby.

RESULTS

J. Barrington lost to G. Alauddin 1-9, 7-9, 10-8, 6-9
P. Ayton lost to Q. Zaman 7-9, 1-9, 4-9
J. Richardson lost to S. Muneer 4-9, 3-9, 9-5, 4-9
J. Easter lost to M. Khan 6-9, 0-9, 0-9
M. Corby lost to M. Yasin 2-9, 9-5, 3-9, 2-9
Pakistan won 5-0

GREAT BRITAIN v PAKISTAN 1974–75

Great Britain and Pakistan played a three-Test series over a period of a month which took in the Amateur Championship. The results as far as Britain was concerned were depressingly predictable, with the Pakistanis exposing the gap in skills between the two countries. Jeff Todhunter at Stockton, Neville Plumley at Brandon Hall, and Mike Palmer at Wembley saw Pakistan take the series 3–0, winning 10 of the 12 matches.

FIRST TEST: STOCKTON

Peter Verow summed it all up: 'I just couldn't get in the game. He carried far too many shots for me and was far too fast about court.'

He was talking about his own match against Mohammed Saleem in the first Test between Great Britain and Pakistan at Stockton YMCA, but his comments could be applied to all but one of the four one-sided rubbers in which the British team were ruthlessly beaten 3–1.

Middlesex's John Richardson salvaged one rubber for Britain, beating the inexperienced Abdul Rahman (drafted in because of Sajjad Muneer's absence) 3–1. Rahman, 21, and on his first tour of Britain, found Richardson's greater tenacity and reliable backhand too much to handle.

Philip Ayton, British No. 1, took a game off British amateur champion Mohibullah Khan, as the latter strung together a series of inexplicable unforced errors. But apart from that game, Ayton, although fighting hard and intelligently, was largely left nonplussed by the mobility and variety of shot with which the world's best amateur confronted him.

Mike Corby, making his first international appearance for three years, crumbled under the merciless pressure of Pakistan's No. 2, Qamar Zaman, whose placements and power swept the Middlesex man off court in less than half an hour. Corby managed only seven points – a true reflection of the immense gap between the two.

Saleem, the 'old man' of the Pakistan team, still had enough energy and skill to spare to deal fairly comfortably with Durham's Verow, at No. 3. Saleem, remarkably mobile, played an attractively ruthless game, varying speed of shot with guile. It was the total counter to Verow's more direct style. Only when Verow took the pace off the ball in the second game, which he won, did he have a chance. But even then, Saleem helped him with some uncharacteristic errors. However, Saleem thereafter stepped up his bewildering mixture of lobs, angles, boasts, and drives, and Verow hardly got a look in.

Perhaps the one frailty of the Pakistan style is its very adventurousness. Unlike the attrition game of the professionals, their imaginative shots leave little room for error, and when pressure is on, or concentration lapses, the errors increase. But sadly the British players are not of the calibre to apply pressure to these super-amateurs.

More heartening for Britain were the reserve matches, in which Kim Bruce-Lockhart and Jonathan Leslie beat Maqsood Ahmed and Atlas Khan respectively. Leslie in particular showed great heart in coming back from 2–1 down to win. His long reach, and willingness to chase apparently lost causes, often helped him out of trouble, but he also showed a brand of courage that augurs well. It was his first international appearance, but it should not be his last.

SECOND TEST: BRANDON HALL

Three stunningly explosive shots from the racket of the newly-crowned amateur champion, Mohibullah Khan, finally severed the thin lifeline to which Great Britain had been clinging in the second Test at the impressive new Brandon Hall club, near Coventry, on 23 December.

As a tremendous cheer from the crowded championship court gallery signalled a 2–1 lead for Philip Ayton against Mohibullah, Peter Verow, Britain's fourth string, was moving to victory over 17-year-old Maqsood Ahmed before only a handful of spectators on an 'outside' court. That put the match level at 1–1 as Mohammed Saleem, the 29-year-old Pakistani captain, had beaten John Richardson in a tense, closely-contested four games in the opening encounter.

Could the rangy, bespectacled Ayton summon the supreme effort of stamina and verve he would need to wrest one more game from Mohibullah, to give his country at least a draw and the faint hope of a win to square the series? The miracle seemed just possible. Ayton, playing with superb control against the demoralising agility and speed of Mohibullah, had brought the faintest hint of a frown to that young man's usually impassive face.

The fourth game began well for Ayton as he moved to 2–0 and continued to keep Mohibullah penned in the back corners. But the Pakistani then got in hand, first drew level and then went to 3–2. There followed four exchanges of service without a score – but these drained the physical reserves on which Ayton had been calling.

Soon afterwards the ball burst, but even this respite was not enough to recharge Ayton's batteries. He managed to get in hand once more, but without scoring, and Mohibullah then ran out to victory 9–2.

Ayton was spent by then, and although he made one final effort early in the fifth, his challenge was visibly receding. Mohibullah then produced three short, vicious, nicked cross-court shots – one to the forehand and two on the backhand – which were struck with such ferocity that they were dead before Ayton was aware that they had even been played.

Richardson, promoted to third string after his achievement of taking Saleem to five games in their amateur championship encounter at Wembley a week earlier, again played with commendable control and maturity against his vastly experienced opponent.

This was illustrated particularly in the first game when he retrieved a 2–6 deficit to go out 9–6 in two hands. Thereafter Saleem, playing drop shots with that gossamer softness that belies his ungainliness about the court, repeatedly stretched Richardson to the front which gradually took its toll. But although he won the next three games he was made to earn the victory, as Richardson lobbed effectively to both wings and kept the rallies tight.

The match between Mike Corby and Qamar Zaman, for all its variety of strokes, had an air of unreality about it. Corby seemed more interested in sharing private exchanges with someone in the gallery than with concentrating on trying to contain Zaman's virtuosity.

Zaman played with the air of a man aware that he could take the match at will. He took risks that he would not have taken in a tighter situation. Not all of them paid off, but enough did to prevent Corby from ever gaining the initiative.

THIRD TEST: WEMBLEY

There was inevitably an air of anti-climax when the two teams came to Wembley for the final Test. Pakistan had already taken a 2–0 winning lead and on this occasion were able to strengthen their team with the inclusion of Sajjad Muneer. Against such a background the British team could be forgiven for feeling that theirs was a hopeless task. Such interest as there was seemed likely to be centred upon Philip Ayton in yet another clash with Mohibullah Khan.

Ayton's form during the first two Tests and the British Amateur Championship touched a new personal peak and perhaps it was reaction to this mammoth effort that led to his swift and disappointing defeat. Certainly the physical and psychological pressures involved when tackling a player of Mohibullah's skill cannot be underestimated. Ayton had previously extended the brilliant Pakistani in a way that only players of real class can expect to do, but any hopes that he would take this a stage further were quickly dashed. Almost immediately, Ayton was on the defensive; he lost the second game to love and gained only two points in the third.

It was the same story for No. 2 man Mike Corby against the brilliant Qamar Zaman. Corby, weary after returning in the early hours of the day from a hockey international, was not in the best condition to do battle with someone of Zaman's sharpness and skill.

The one match where Britain might have expected a victory was Peter Verow against Mohammed Saleem. Verow's form, vastly improved, gave rise to some hope of an upset at the expense of the slightly vulnerable older Saleem.

Verow began well, but narrowly lost the first game 10–9. When the second also escaped him 9–6 it seemed that he was on his way to defeat. The third, however, revealed all of Verow's fighting qualities and the recovery unsettled Saleem, pushing him into a series of unforced errors. Having taken that game 9–7, Verow took advantage of his newly-won initiative to level the match at 2–2 in the fourth, and it was now a question of whether his physical reserves would be sufficient to finish the job.

In the event they were not, but Verow's brave rally was the high spot of a sad evening for Britain.

Muneer, although not match fit and made to work harder than he might have expected, dealt comfortably with John Richardson in four games.

RESULTS

FIRST TEST

Stockton YMCA, 7 December 1974

1 Philip Ayton lost to Mohibullah Khan 3-9, 9-5, 4-9, 2-9
2 Mike Corby lost to Qamar Zaman 1-9, 3-9, 3-9
3 Peter Verow lost to Mohammed Saleem 6-9, 9-1, 5-9, 3-9
4 John Richardson bt Abdul Rahman 9-3, 9-4, 7-9, 9-2
Pakistan won 3-1

SECOND TEST *(sponsored by Falcon Inns Limited)*

Brandon Hall, Coventry, 23 December 1974

1 Philip Ayton lost to Mohibullah Khan 5-9, 9-7, 9-7, 2-9, 0-9
2 Mike Corby lost to Qamar Zaman 7-9, 5-9, 7-9
3 Peter Verow bt Maqsood Ahmed 9-2, 9-4, 0-9, 9-3
4 John Richardson lost to Mohammed Saleem 9-6, 5-9, 7-9, 6-9
Pakistan won 3-1

THIRD TEST

Wembley Squash Centre, 7 January 1975

1 Philip Ayton lost to Mohibullah Khan 4-9, 0-9, 2-9
2 Mike Corby lost to Qamar Zaman 5-9, 4-9, 6-9
3 Peter Verow lost to Mohammed Saleem 9-10, 6-9, 9-7, 9-2, 4-9
4 John Richardson lost to Sajjad Muneer 6-9, 9-4, 5-9, 9-2
Pakistan won 4-0

PAKISTAN REIGN SUPREME

Dicky Rutnagur

In the 1950s, when Hashim Khan reigned supreme for seven years and was then succeeded by three others of his clan – Roshan, Azam, and Mohibullah – it was hard to imagine that the British Open title, acknowledged as the world's championship, would ever leave Pakistan. The Khan dynasty ruled, and ruled absolutely, for 13 years, a period half as long as the whole history of the British Open up to that point. During that era, Pakistan and the Khans also provided the losing finalist on nine occasions.

Then 11 years elapsed before another Pathan (the race of the Khans), Qamar Zaman, won the British Open – last season. Zaman, no doubt, was a surprise winner. But it was not all that unlikely that the title should have been won by Pakistan, for several of their younger players had worked towards this goal for five years with burning zeal and total dedication.

The result of their endeavours is reflected in the following statistics of the 1974–75 British Open: the finalists were both Pakistani; three of them figured in the semi-finals, four in the quarters, and as many as seven survived to the last 16.

Zaman's hold on the British Open title ranks him as the world's number one. But in my book, Geoff Hunt is still the most consistent match-winner in contemporary squash. However, if an international team championship was to be staged today, Pakistan would almost certainly win it, and win it at a canter.

It is ironical that except for India and, perhaps, Egypt, Pakistan has the barest facilities for cultivating squash champions of the remaining member countries of the International Squash Rackets Federation. Courts are few in relation to the population, and they are scattered among the principal cities and the big military establishments. If not the property of the armed forces, these courts belong to clubs whose subscription would probably exceed the average national income. Rackets of even indigenous manufacture are beyond the reach of the man in the street. In other words, squash in Pakistan is the game of the *élite* or the services.

The Pakistani players who grace the British circuit today are domiciled in various parts of the country. But all except Gogi Alauddin and Sajjad Muneer (both Punjabis from Lahore) are Pathans, a tribe of frontiermen with strong ethnic characteristics of the Afghans. Their original homes are in the villages near Peshawar, the town at the Pakistan end of the historic Khyber Pass. The nature of the terrain they live in (rocky and mountainous) and the extremes of climate make the Pathans a tough race, both temperamentally and physically. They are impulsive and yet they have the highlanders' native cunning which must serve them well in squash.

Where, you might ask, did the Pathans come to discover the game of squash? All sport on the sub-continent that holds India and Pakistan has a common origin – the British Army. Every cantonment had, and still has, its club. Even the smaller military establishments boasted some sort of sporting facilities to go with the officers' mess, invariably a squash court.

A frontier posting was no holiday in the sun. Action was never far away and sporting pursuits were less leisurely than at camps further south. This is one probable explanation for the higher popularity of squash in this region.

As I said, clubs and messes all had squash courts (most of which were open to the sky and had concrete flooring), and in some instances, rackets courts as well. The clubs recruited their staff from neighbouring villages and many of them lived with their families within the grounds of these imperial institutions.

While the *sahibs* were at work and the *memsahibs* played mah-jong, the staff had the run of the courts. Some of them developed quite a skill at racket games, so that if a member arrived at the club and found that his arranged opponent had been called to duty or had caught the sun, he could always find a butler or a gardener's son to give him a game.

The most exceptionally talented among them became tennis, rackets, and squash professionals. They were such natural ball players that they could switch from one game to the other at the drop of a hat. Some built-in mechanism seemed to make the necessary adjustments in technique and timing. If there were no vacancies for professionals in the Peshawar area, they sought their fortunes further afield. Jobs available were advertised by word of mouth and would be filled just as quickly as a train could travel from Peshawar to wherever the young man was needed to serve.

I don't know why I talk of the system in the past tense, because although it may have become a bit more refined now, the basic pattern has not changed. Even Mohibullah Khan, the present holder of the British Amateur Championship, started as a tennis ballboy, not so very long ago.

The circumstances under which Hashim Khan, the greatest squash player of all time, came to the game were not much different. That was exactly half a century ago.

Hashim's father was chief steward at the Peshawar Army Club. Each afternoon, after school, Hashim walked to the club, sat on the back wall of the *al fresco* and watched the members at play with utter fascination. When the ball flew out of court, Hashim ran down to retrieve it, and as he said himself, he performed this operation as fast as he could because he was eager to watch the next rally.

For his troubles, Hashim was paid Rs.5 (which must have been worth about 10 shillings in those days) a month. But this payment Hashim looked on as only a bonus. His true reward, as far as he was concerned, was the chance to get on court with his friends when the members had called it a day.

Hashim imagined he was the luckiest, happiest little boy alive when tragedy struck. His father was killed in a road accident under his very eyes. Thus at 11 Hashim was the man of the house. His mother could persuade him to stay on at school for only a few months afterwards. A combination of a sense of domestic responsibility and his complete fascination with squash made up his mind for him. No more school. Henceforth learning was to be on the squash court. Practice on his own took the place of those enjoyable games with his young contemporaries.

The rough edges were smoothed out by the son of the senior pro, who was also his assistant. While he learnt the game, Hashim scraped up a living as ballboy, giving the odd member a game when the resident professionals were not available, and by re-stringing rackets. Although he could play with a member for a tip, the strict professional code prevented Hashim from giving instruction. However, he did have one pupil – his kid brother, Azam. He taught Azam every game he played himself, and though the younger Khan became a squash legend himself in due course, his first love was tennis.

Hashim's was a long apprenticeship. He was in his mid-twenties before he got his first post as senior professional, at the RAF mess in Peshawar. And he was approaching middle age when he made his first and successful bid for the British Open title, in 1950.

Pakistan was by then an independent country, and Hashim was now in the service of the Royal Pakistan Air Force. It had not occurred to him to play in the British Open for the simple reason that he did not know that he was good enough to do so. Hashim's eyes were opened by the participation in 1949 of a younger cousin, Abdul Bari, who worked on the other side of the border, at the Cricket Club of India in Bombay. A converted tennis player, Bari volleyed strongly and played a deceptive drop shot with a lovely touch. At his first attempt, Bari reached the final of the British Open.

But whenever they met on home soil, Hashim always

Mohibullah Khan arrived in Britain in 1971 and immediately won the Drysdale Cup. One knew even then that a star was in the ascendant.

had the better of Bari, and Hashim now knew that new horizons were open to him. Thus the next year he won the championship. He dropped a mere five points – all in one game – while winning the final against the celebrated Mahmoud El Karim, of Egypt, the inimitable stylist who had won every British Open since the war.

Hashim won the title six more times. There was just one break in the sequence of wins, brought about by his cousin, Roshan. Then the mantle of champion fell on Azam Khan, who had started to play serious squash only months before he made his first British Open appearance and reached the final.

Azam was champion four times, and was then succeeded by Mohibullah Khan, his sister's son. Several other Pathans played in the British Open during that era and although their names never found a place on the roll of honour, they all made for high quality entertainment.

As a country, Pakistan was less than three years old when Hashim first won the British Open and it meant a lot to the young nation to have a world champion. He came home to a hero's welcome. He was given money, a plot of land, the inevitable gold watch, and a commissioned rank in the air force. They even named a railway station after him. Considering that he was almost 30 before he started to take home a worthwhile wage packet, these were riches. Still, when he received an offer in 1960 to go to America, he could not resist it. Nor did Pakistan try to stop him going.

Hashim was 44, and he had given to Pakistan squash all he had to give as player and as a source of inspiration. Moreover, the American game would, at his age, be easier on his legs. Not only had he shaped a future for the game in Pakistan, but sparked off a squash boom in Australia following his exhibition tour there in 1951.

There was, at the time Hashim left Pakistan, a heavy exodus of Pathan professionals towards the West. Azam had already gone to the New Grampian Club in London. Abdul Bari came to the Junior Carlton, Nazrullah Khan to the Lansdowne. Mohibullah also went to America. The list is far from complete and only Roshan Khan, among the big names, stayed behind.

With the stars all living abroad and out of the limelight of competitive play, interest in squash waned in Pakistan. Only one man, Aftab Jawaid, made any impact. But Jawaid was an attritional player and much too staid a character to stir the imagination.

Perhaps the establishment of the World Amateur Championship in 1966 served to revive enthusiasm. On that occasion, Gogi Alauddin, then only 16, gave initial promise of becoming the player he is now. When the competition was next held in England, in 1968, Gogi impressed again while Sajjad Muneer and Mohammed Saleem also caught the eye.

Of course, the modern messiah of squash, Jonah Barrington, had to be involved somewhere in the course of events that brought Pakistan squash back to prominence. The ebullient Irishman made two trips in close succession to Pakistan, the second with a troupe of international stars whom he had himself brought together.

During his travels, Jonah paid a visit to Khan country. You can imagine the prestige of a world squash champion in a district which itself had bred more than one. He was accorded a welcome such as the Pathans would give one of their own heroic sons. With customary fervour, Jonah said that Peshawar was his spiritual home, for it was from two noble Khans, Nazrullah and Azam, that he had learnt his craft.

The younger players were reminded of their heritage and duly inspired. The presence of the visiting stars also impressed on them that new horizons were opening before the successful squash player, promising a congenial life of travel and profitable returns.

Unfortunately, personal ambition was resented by the establishment. There was a lot of in-fighting within the Pakistan SRA. Suspensions fell on players, like death sentences after an unsuccessful political coup. Those in particular disfavour were Alauddin, Muneer, and Hiddy Jahan, all of them residents of Lahore, owing allegiance to the Punjab Association. Ironically, it was this trio who made Pakistan's presence felt again in big-time squash abroad. They made annual trips to Britain and Australia, played in as many tournaments as they could, and became better players from one day to the next.

Gogi twice won the British Amateur prior to turning professional; while Hiddy, with his virile and eye-catching style, became one of the game's personalities. Both of them came from a squash background, their fathers (by whom they were taught) being professionals. They grew up in the atmosphere of the game, and worked at it in the age-old manner.

Although immensely talented, it was a bit different for Sajjad Muneer. He had to reconcile his enthusiasm for the game with his studies for an engineering degree. Sajjad has had to be content with less than a full-time squash career, and without equalling the success of his compatriots, has left no doubt about his class.

In the spring of 1971, Pakistan sent out another Khan, Mohibullah, to play in the Drysdale Cup, the British Junior Championship. He was only 15 or 16 then, but he won it quite comfortably and one knew even then that a new star was in the ascendant. A little more sudden was the emergence of Qamar Zaman, who husbanded his remarkable flair with newly-acquired discipline to lift last season's British Open title.

Needless to say, Zaman was also reared in a family of professionals. He is a nephew of Aftab Jawaid and therefore a grandson of Zen Khan, who was rackets champion of Pakistan. Not distantly related are Mohamed Yasin, the 1974 British Open finalist, and Mohammed Saleem.

Mohibullah and Zaman both decided on professional careers in April 1975. Thus it seems likely that all the big names will be living, or at least spending most of their time, abroad.

Will their absence set the game back in Pakistan as happened after the departure of the first generation of stars? It is less likely, for after the upheavals of a few years ago, the Pakistan SRA's house is in better order and government, having realised that the country is an endless source of talent, has set itself to put the game on a sounder, broader base.

At the forefront of the scheme to modernise the machine that turns out squash stars at an enviable rate is Air Marshal Nur Khan, a keen squash player, who is Chairman of Pakistan International Airlines.

Playing an important role, no doubt, in shaping the destiny of Pakistan squash will be the genial Sheryar Khan, another squash fanatic, who was until last spring the Counsellor at the Pakistan Embassy in London. Now he is back in Islamabad for a spell at the foreign office.

Dicky Rutnagur is squash correspondent of The Daily Telegraph.

AROUND THE WORLD

Robert Jolly

There is a squash boom going on. This is one of the media's favourite clichés, but it is also a fact. People are changing their leisure activities and many of them are turning to squash. There is scant data for extravagant international claims, but high growth-rates in terms of players and court building are apparent in many parts of the world. Britain is the melting-pot for enterprises in the playing, manufacturing, court-building, and administrative aspects of the sport.

With a growth-rate of approximately 30 per cent in the playing arena, and expansion of products – such as rackets – running at around 25 per cent per annum, there are wide opportunities for new companies to buy into the boom; especially as existing manufacturers are unable to cope with the magnitude of the game's growth. Goudie Squash International has made a recent and spectacular entry into squash after studying this situation; Sondico and Darbrook, importers of Indian sports goods, recently brought out rackets aimed at the upper end of the market; and Gola, famous in shoes, have moved into supplying squash equipment.

The 1974–75 season in Britain has been severely hampered by a shortage of squash balls. The demands, formerly met by the Dunlop factory, have grown in staggering proportions and a new £80,000 plant is under construction to help cope with the situation. But the short-term 'squeeze' has prompted several manufacturers to try to unravel the problem of developing a new type of ball. Up to now production has remained a tight oligopoly, testimony to the difficulty of finding a ball which, in layman's language, will 'bounce right'.

Court building grows apace, although the prolonged economic gloom in Britain has curtailed the profit opportunities for many commercial enterprises. The initial capital outlay in court construction is growing monthly – adding about 30 per cent each year for the same court. The cost of borrowed money has deterred many, and yet the growth persists.

One of the major areas of expansion has been in the addition of courts to already established sporting clubs to combine, for example, with football, rugby, or tennis.

Many such clubs, faced with financial problems, have seen revenue from squash as something of a salvation. Public centres operated by local authorities, and courts added to works sports and social clubs, are more than making up for any slackening off in the realm of private enterprise.

Australian court growth took a different path in its pioneering days, but today, as in Britain, the average viable number of courts in a centre is eight. Not long ago the standard squash complex consisted of only four. Although the heyday of the Australian squash boom has passed, steady growth continues as new courts spring up in the outer suburbs of the cities. The older, inner city centres are going through a transitional stage to make their usage more intensive. The Australian market is ripe for new products and an enlarged tournament circuit. However, the immense distances involved in travelling and covering the country make it difficult to initiate both of these areas successfully.

The Swedish squash scene can be regarded as a barometer of the continent. Squash growth, having begun in the 1930s, went through a long period of stagnation until the late 1960s, when the game's popularity increased once more.

The kings of Swedish squash built empires out of nothing: they sold the sport and an atmosphere: they sold a leisure activity and a trend. They knew that the trend would

Qamar Zaman (left) and Geoff Hunt, two of the major stars whose performances throughout the world act as an inspirational force to the growth of the game.

result in people actually playing the game, and after that the game would recommend itself. One such empire is the Intersquash Company which was launched on the endeavor of Jan Landvik and Jan Hansen, while Carl Kindal, who now controls the largest group of courts in Sweden, runs his own publicity-shy organisation. These forces combined to draw new blood into the sport. Court building continues today but the garnering of profits is progressively more difficult, as efforts to increase the playing population meet opposition from economy-concious potential customers.

The result of this situation where court building is pressing (or has pressed) ahead of the growth in numbers of players, is that clubs often poach groups of players away from rivals. Thus more time and energy are spent on wooing the existing squash player than on attracting the novice.

Just as the success of Swedish squash court operations in the early seventies was achieved by supreme marketing, the remedy for the present tempered growth is the same.

The rapid expansion of squash in Finland followed the Swedish example, but continues unabated. Strangely, Norway is devoid of squash save for a rumoured single court installed on a farm for private use; and the Danes, whose hard-core of enthusiasts rival the most evangelical of all squash followers, have been unable to really break loose from the Copenhagen Club located in the heart of the city. A recently constructed centre some 40 kilometres north of Copenhagen has not been an immediate success.

The nation likely to step into the limelight in terms of the squash boom is Holland. A steady increase in the number of clubs has occurred over the past two years. Presently, many private developers and giants such as the EMI company are ready to build dozens of courts.

The plans and aspirations for West German development are extensive. The most important progress being made currently is the new complex under construction in Hamburg. Backing this centre are many of the leading names in German squash, the men who have travelled European squash circles and have mapped out their future success, starting in Hamburg.

The expensive Montparnasse Club in Paris is establishing itself after a year, although there are few signs of rivals for the moment.

In Brussels, however, the Castle Club is open, which joins the Leopold, and plans are prepared for further expansion.

Switzerland and Spain are on the launching pad ready for lift-off, which leaves Austria and Portugal outside the excitement.

The situation in Greece is perhaps best described as 'fluid'. Much groundwork had been done to win governmental approval, but since then the change in leadership necessitates renewed efforts.

In Africa, Nigeria pushes ahead with squash development. The administration seems well coordinated and the competitions soundly organised. No doubt the interest of General Gowon, the head of State, influences the rising popularity.

The first public centre in South Africa, in the Transvaal, is the precursor of numerous other shemes. The success of the centre owes a great deal to the men behind it, the Barrow brothers and Simon Malone, whose hearts really lie in the game.

London is not the only place making news with a championship court. In Salisbury, Rhodesia, a huge monument to championship play was built last year to hold a capacity crowd of 800. In Karachi, too, there are plans for a grandiose championship complex to house major tournaments of worldwide stature. With such depth of playing talent this appears an appropriate venture.

Further east, the sport flourishes too. Japanese squash was not able to explode in quite the manner that was first indicated, but it has taken a strong foothold, and these enterprising people will find a way to realise their dream of thousands of courts.

In the Philippines, however, squash has captured the imagination of many, and solid media exposure has resulted. This, in turn, has stimulated greater player response. The tour of players of the calibre of Zaman and Mohibullah provides fresh impetus to the growing legion in Manilla.

The American continent seems to have resisted the temptation to construct courts of international dimensions, but the growth in the number of courts of their own size continues. Commercially run courts are creeping into the USA whilst they have created a fever of activity in Mexico.

From every corner of the globe comes news of squash on the boil – new courts, new players, new ideas. There is a silent revolution going on. Some areas are becoming involved more rapidly than others, but everywhere you turn, squash is putting fact behind the media's cliché – there *is* a Squash Boom going on.

SQUASH AND TELEVISION

Robert Jolly

It has taken a long time to penetrate, but the squash message appears to be hitting home as far as the media are concerned. The reluctance on the part of television and national newspapers to give screen time and space to squash is gradually being worn away, albeit slowly. Ironically, it was the lack-lustre, almost disastrous exhibition between Geoff Hunt and Jonah Barrington which the BBC televised early in 1974 that gave the impetus for mass exposure of the game. It wasn't the best squash in the world, but many viewers took the trouble to write to the BBC and express their appreciation. The viewers clearly wanted more.

The important thing was that the subject of squash and television was now being tackled in a serious fashion, and the BBC were sufficiently encouraged to stay with the game and improve their presentation.

The opening of the Wembley centre with its built-in camera positions and high standard lighting has provided television with a ready-made home. The BBC went there in February for the final of the 1974–75 British Open and pronounced that they were more than satisfied with the facilities. How much Wembley will actually be used by television is debatable. There is no confirmed slot for squash in the programming of BBC sport over 1975–76, and although this does not mean that squash will not be seen during that time, it does reflect the still slightly sceptical view of the game held within the Corporation.

The attitude of independent companies will have an important bearing. Thames Television have already screened a series of instructional films and the approach of some regional stations, such as Granada TV, Anglia TV, and Southern TV could almost be described as enlightened. Player interviews and news items about squash have been televised and if this kind of treatment continues it will surely act as a spur to those producers or sports editors who are waiting to be convinced.

Anglia conducted an interesting experiment with a special match between Jonah Barrington and the man he deposed as world champion, the Egyptian Abou Taleb. This one-off affair, played at Gunnerslade's Chelmsford Club under special rules devised by managing director

John Griffiths, is planned to be the forerunner of a television series. Bernard Howson, sports editor of Anglia, regarded the session of squash as 'transmittable'. 'We are going to edit it a little more and insert some slow motion film into the mainstream of the match. I think we did reasonably well in covering the game. All the facilities were right. The blue floor was fine, and when the squash is finally edited and transmitted we will monitor the response and see what we can do for the sport.'

While the 'wait and see' attitude persists with competition squash coverage, the instructional aspect is growing with the news that the Westward and Channel Islands networks have bought the instructional series screened by Thames. No one has as yet, however, sold a purpose-built training and coaching film specially made for television.

The BBC went to Wembley for the final of the 1974–75 British Open, and were more than satisfied with the facilities.

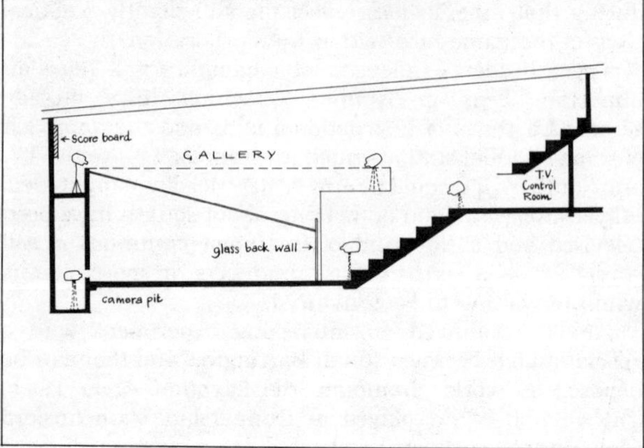

The opening of Wembley has provided television with a ready-made home. Illustrated are the camera positions.

If squash continues to receive this kind of exposure, it will help the 'selling' of championship play both to viewers, who will understand the game better, and to the television programme planners.

The next landmark in the development of squash as a spectator sport will be a follow-up to the introduction of the glass back wall, with side walls and/or part of the front wall made of a substance through which spectators can see. The material's surface will of course have to produce a normal bounce of the ball.

Television coverage in Australia was up to its usual standards in both live and filmed reports of the Australian championships. The recent introduction of a glass back wall in Melbourne meant that the cameras caught the action from the same position favoured by the Anglia crew in their tests. The effect from viewing through the wall was highly recommended and this does cast some doubt on the BBC's basic vantage point some distance away from the court, looking over the wall rather than through it.

One of the spin-offs from the growing tournament circuit is the stimulus being provided by increasing prize-money and the development of personalities among the leading players. These factors have given newspapers and local radio the basis for giving squash much-needed mileage. The interest which this creates will help to pressurise television into giving more coverage.

Jonah Barrington (left) and Philip Ayton in action during the Amateurs v Professionals match to inaugurate Wembley, which the BBC televised.

TOMMY STEELE HOLDS COURT

Ian Keresey

It was not one of Tommy Steele's best matinées. An audience which can only be kindly described as 'scattered' began to filter from the auditorium before the performance was over. The top entertainer was clearly struggling to find the right chord; his footwork was ungainly, his timing weak, and his execution slack. Only an occasional comment from that familiar Cockney voice brought a faint tremor of laughter from the spectators.

In truth, this was not Tommy Steele attempting to entertain West End theatregoers in his latest show, but Tommy Steele the squash fanatic having a gruelling work-out on the championship court at Wembley's national centre with Samir Nadim, the top Egyptian professional and coach.

Tommy stayed on court an hour, and underwent a strenuous test of endurance which would have left an ordinary mortal stranded, gasping for breath, as the track-suited Nadim constantly placed the ball tantalisingly within range but always just that important fraction out of reach.

At last the entertainer took himself off court and was delighted to find that his opponent had one or two beads of perspiration on his forehead. He remarked on the fact and Nadim smilingly replied: 'Stick to the game and you will one day make me remove my track suit.'

After showering and changing in a small private dressing-room – 'I am class you know', explained Tommy with that familiar twinkle in his blue eyes – he gulped down two sugared coffees and a ham sandwich, and then talked about his introduction to squash and his subsequent addiction to the game.

'About 11 months ago I moved into an old house near Richmond in Surrey and it had a squash court attached. At the time I never even knew what the game was all about, let alone played it,' he reflected. 'I thought, right, I'll give the game a go and if I don't like it then I'll have a swimming pool put there instead.'

Typically, Tommy approached squash with the same energy he has put into his stage career, giving the game everything he had to offer. His first lesson was at the Lansdowne Club in London. 'I was shown how to hold

Tommy Steele plays squash with the same energy he has put into his stage career. If he can, he likes to play six days a week.

the racket correctly, which might sound rather basic but at least that stops any bad habits forming from the start.' Progress was slow at first, under the tuition of Rehmat Khan, then Australian Charlie Booth, but Tommy adapted quickly, found he was enjoying himself, and soon learned the technique of playing drop shots and volleying to a length.

Three months of lessons took him across London, to the New Grampians Club in Shepherds Bush and the guidance of Azam Khan. 'He taught me how to tighten up my game.' Apart from receiving coaching, Tommy also plays matches against other members of the New Grampian. 'There are about 400 names on the ladder. I was fortunate enough to go in about number 12 and have progressed to fourth place', he said proudly. 'My immediate ambition is to win a place in their first team and then perhaps reach county standard. Who knows, in a few years time I might win the Veterans' Championship.' That is no mean programme for the hard working 38-year-old entertainer who began playing squash weighing 11st 4lb and has dramatically dropped to a rather underweight 10st 2lb.

He only puffs two cigars a day, does not touch alcohol, and likes to play six days a week, with one day's rest. That is usually a day when he gives two performances at the theatre (he has been starring in *Hans Andersen* at the London Palladium).

Tommy's philosophy for the game has a hard edge, and could well have a great deal to do with his success in the tough world of show business. 'I go on court to win and nothing gives me greater pleasure than to see my opponent rushing to the nearest tap to cool himself down after a game. That might sound a little callous but I must be honest about what I say and think.

'Squash is a fascinating game. I have played other sports, soccer in my younger days, but the nearest equivalent to it must be snooker, rather than the obvious choices like tennis and badminton, the other popular racket games.

'I don't mind telling you that I know a little bit about snooker and, like squash, it is all about angles and leaving the ball where your opponent has no chance to play it constructively.'

It appears that not too many other show business personalities play squash. 'John Cleese (*Monty Python*) is pretty good and learned the game at university; film actor Robert Shaw plays a bit I believe, and I have had a game or two with Anthony Valentine (*Colditz*). There aren't too many other well known people who go in for such rigorous work-outs but the game has certainly caught on among the everyday working folk in this country of ours.

'Just look at this centre here', and at that Tommy gazed expansively out across the courts. 'A future world class player is probably playing here at this very moment. I don't know his name, and you don't know his name, but that's because he is only 9 or 10 years old. One day though, he will be at the top of the sport and we shall all recognise and admire him.'

Talk of a generation of budding prospects soon led to his views on the current crop of top players. 'I was fortunate enough to watch part of the British Open Championship this year and, to be frank, admired all the professionals in action, particularly the foreign ones.'

Did he think Qamar Zaman of Pakistan a worthy champion? 'Obviously he is a great player but I cannot help thinking that he happened to be the best of the bunch only during that particular tournament. Everything went right for him but had the championship been played the following week maybe one of the others would have been

A touch of artistry can be put into this game too . . .

in commanding form. My point is that I don't believe there is much to choose between any of them. They are all simply brilliant.'

What about the British players? 'Well, apart from Jonah Barrington we are just not in the same league. We don't seem to have any team spirit. I remember that every time I watched a Pakistan player or an Australian or an Egyptian in action once the match was over, win or lose, he would immediately be joined by some of his fellow countrymen and his performance would be analysed. Did you ever see that happening to a British player? Not on your life. They went on court, played, showered then probably went home. With that sort of attitude there is no way Britain can get back to the top in the world game.

'I think the way to create a better climate for our own players is simple. Instead of a sponsor putting up a lot of prize-money for some obscure tournament, he should use it to pay for the board and lodgings of our players. That way the player does not have to worry where the next meal will be coming from or go to work before an important match. Instead, he can dedicate himself to the game.'

Tommy does not only want to extract as much as he can from squash for his personal benefit. He also aims to put a great deal back. He has a scheme to build a big squash complex in the London area very shortly, along similar lines to Wembley. But he promised: 'If it happens then I will make sure that one court is always available for our best amateurs and professionals to practise on, free of charge. That may be only a small contribution but our players deserve every facility possible.'

I left the tousled-haired entertainer standing alone on the balcony overlooking number eight court. He was watching two football-shirted youngsters, wearing baseball boots and using borrowed rackets in a brave attempt to master the game. I had the distinct impression that the swimming pool once scheduled for his beautiful Surrey home could not have been further from his mind.

Ian Keresey is a sports writer for the Press Association.

SQUASH FOR THE OVER-FORTIES

Dr J. L. Blonstein

Squash is the ideal form of exercise. It gives the maximum exercise in the minimum time, can be played in any weather, day or night, and is a comparatively cheap game to play. It keeps the muscles contracting which, in turn, press on the blood-vessels and ensure a good circulation. It 'shakes up' the liver, improving digestion, while mental stresses and anxieties are forgotten on the court. The increased perspiration rids the body of harmful toxins.

The over-forties who have not played squash before would, in my opinion, be unwise to start at that age. At 40 and over the muscles and ligaments are not so supple, joints begin showing signs of wear and tear (early arthritis), and response to violent exercise may result in breathlessness or even distress. For a game to do any good you should generate a good sweat and a pulse rate of 120.

The over-40 starter may reach this stage but suffer personal distress. His ligaments will have become slack and somewhat frayed, and hence ruptured Achilles' tendon, a tennis leg (where muscle fibres of the calf muscles are torn), a Charley Horse injury where muscle fibres of the hamstring muscles (back of the thighs) are torn, and slipped discs, become more likely.

Before deciding to take up squash after the age of 40, have your blood-pressure and an electro-cardiograph of your heart taken. If you are given a clean bill of health, then play only for exercise and not competitively. Many over-forties find that they are overweight, feel sluggish, and become breathless on exertion. They hope to reduce their weight by playing squash. Some players lose as much as two pounds in weight after a game, but two pints of beer or two whiskies will restore the pre-playing weight. Those of you over 40 who want to reduce weight should cut down on starchy foods (bread, potatoes, puddings, pastry, and sweet things) and fried foods: but you can eat meat, fish, fruit, and green vegetables. Alcohol is very rich in calories and should be taken in moderation. Don't use a lift if you can walk up the stairs. Exercises suitable for the over-forties are running (not sprinting), jogging, brisk walking, pedal-cycling, swimming, and golf. Those over-forties who are still playing squash will also benefit by these exercises, which help to disperse excessive cholesterol in the blood and tone up the muscles.

Those who have played from youth, but experience pain in the middle of the chest or excessive breathlessness should have their hearts examined. Some squash players are concerned that they might 'strain their hearts' while playing the game. This is a complete fallacy. There is no such thing as the 'athletic heart' or 'heart strain'.

In violent exercises all the organs and functions concerned are exposed to considerable stress but the healthy heart has a margin of safety that precludes 'strain', an injury or excessive tension when the heart is stretched beyond its normal limits. The use of the term 'heart strain' is encouraged by the appearance of a player suffering extreme exhaustion during and after the game. There may be distortion and pinching of the face, gasping for breath, cold perspiration and a weak rapid pulse, nausea, vomiting (rarely), and faintness. These distressing symptoms do not indicate cardiac failure. Exhaustion after a match is due to the adrenalin and sugar in the blood being completely used up. Lack of food for some hours, mental worry, or an infection (e.g. a cold) are possible causes, and psychological factors such as being highly strung, or the urge to win, are often important.

At the beginning of an exercise period the healthy heart dilates in order to increase the efficiency of contraction of the individual muscle fibres. Slight dilatation helps the heart to empty itself completely at each beat. On cessation of exercise the heart diminishes in size and is restored to normal. As a result of training and regular exercise, the fibres of the heart muscle enlarge with their capillaries so that the heart muscle receives an increased blood supply with greater efficiency. This enlargement (known medically as hypertrophy) is not pathological in any way.

If you have a healthy heart, no form of exercise can damage or strain it. If heart symptoms appear during or after a game of squash there must have been some existing heart disease which would have caused a breakdown even after the slightest effort. The very rare death at squash occurs only in those players whose hearts are already damaged as a result of congenital or previous disease.

The over-forties who are regular players will want to know when to give up the game. The time comes when you feel excessively tired after a game and when you find yourself losing your mobility.

They say that life begins at 40, but don't start squash at 40 unless you take the precautions I have mentioned. For those over 40 who have been playing since their youth or early twenties, I advise them to go on playing and enjoying the game – it will help to keep them fit.

Dr J. L. Blonstein is Hon. Medical Adviser to the Squash Rackets Association.

SQUASH FOR FITNESS

John Hopkins

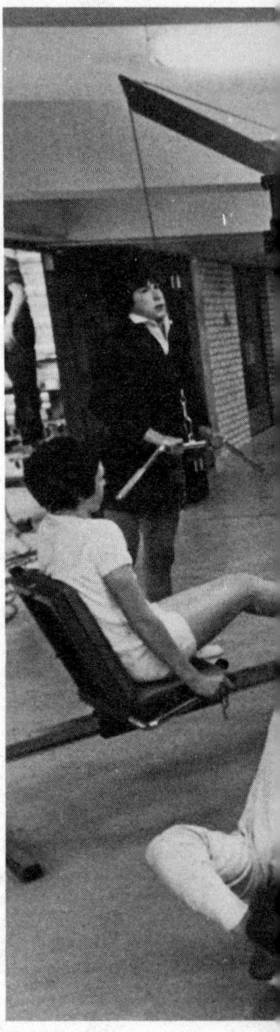

It has taken a century and a quarter, and it has cost a good many pounds both sterling and *avoirdupois*, but we have at last twigged that bashing a little black ball around in a white-walled court is one of the best ways yet discovered of combining exercise and pleasure.

Squash does not take long, doesn't cost much, is more interesting than running, and for most hard-working men and women it is ideal for keeping in shape. Yet for years the Americans dismissed it as, variously, a vegetable, a soft drink, and a game for effete Ivy League East Coasters. In Britain, too, it had a social cachet that smacked of social privilege, along with polo, croquet, and Eton fives.

Not until the 1960s, when personal health and fitness became a matter of national concern; not until President John Kennedy formed the President's Council of Physical Fitness and Sports in the USA; not until heart attacks and associated diseases became the biggest killing illness known to mankind; not until then did anyone pay more than passing interest to squash.

In America, the swing to personal fitness was led by a middle-aged, portly man who began jogging to recover his health after a heart attack. Subsequently a book on the subject became a bestseller, as did one issued by the Canadian Air Force listing exercises that could be done in a few minutes morning and night. Quickly it spread across the Atlantic. The Danes organised runs through the woods on the edge of Copenhagen. Parisians ran through the Bois de Boulogne every Sunday afternoon, thousands of them, streaming along at their own rate, walking or trotting, with nobody to hustle them. Health farms sprang up in Britain and customers paid £5 to lose one pound. Yoga went from being a fad to a phenomenon.

And then up popped an Irishman with a Biblical name, an eloquent turn of phrase, and a fetish for fitness. For years Jonah Barrington gave up girls. He ran miles every morning – and miles every evening. He eschewed parties. Though he lived in London he might as well have been in a lighthouse for all the socialising he did. And, as a result, he became world champion.

In 1972 he forecast to a friend that in Britain squash would be the leisure sport of the eighties. He was wrong.

England international Ian Nuttall (right) putting himself, and pupils of St Peter's School, York, through a tough session of physical training – the sort of programme that has helped him become one of the country's top amateurs.

Helped by his example, squash was on its way to becoming the leisure sport of the seventies. Stockbrokers furled their umbrellas, tilted their bowlers, and walked to work – with a squash racket sticking out of their briefcases. Mothers in track suits delivered their children to school with squash rackets on the back seat of the car. Lunch time became squash time. Dinner time became squash time. By 1975 an accurate assessment of the growth of the game was that in the previous 10 years it had grown 10 times over until it was played by 500,000 people: one in every 100 of the population.

The game is no cure-all, however. It might not appeal to everybody. It doesn't provide the open air and sense of freedom of golf or the sea, nor the tranquillity of fishing. But it does in a very short time shake up one's liver – the body's thermometer – shake down one's calorie intake and induce a feeling of good, honest, all-over fatigue. And this it does for everybody, from the best to the worst.

A club player put it perfectly when he said 'to walk back to the dressing-room as weak as a kitten with the sweat dripping off but with your mind as clear as tomorrow's dawn is better than five reefers or a trip on LSD. There are no hang-ups.'

Four American doctors endorsed the game again recently, as a means of promoting health. 'Excellent for endurance' said one. 'Excellent on almost all counts because of the agility it promotes' said a second. A third pointed out that 'when played properly it provides a maximum of exercise in a minimum of time'. The fourth noted that it was an endurance game and then estimated that one 'could lose 1,000 calories per hour by playing it'. Of the 14 sports the doctors were assessing, which included bicycling, tennis, golf, and ice-skating, squash was reckoned one of the best.

For most players its benefits far exceed its deficiencies. For them it doesn't matter that it is always played indoors and that the lighting varies enormously from one court to another. Nor does it matter that occasionally, an opponent may let slip his racket or, simply, lose his temper. 'To my mind it has everything. It exercises all the main muscle groups of the body', says Jonah Barrington's coach Bomber Harris, who is now a full-time coach after a number of years as a physical training instructor in the RAF. 'The body is kept virtually in a crouch (or should be) so the quadruceps are being used all the time. You have to bend to hit and stretch to volley, which is good for your abdominals. And don't forget the weight of the racket in your hand and how that strengthens the wrist and forearm.'

Rod Laver's left forearm is so much bigger than his right that he has to do exercises to strengthen the weaker one. By the same token squash players tend to be strong in the leg but relatively weak above the waist. That doesn't bother Bomber. 'It is a game where there is no relaxation', he says enthusiastically. 'It is far better than tennis where you can get bored because it goes on for so long. Besides, tennis is more of a strength game and the big bloke with the crashing serve is at an advantage. You don't have to be strong in squash, nor very fast for that matter. Yet the eventual winner has to be fit and, from the health point of view, he can only do himself good by playing. In a hard game you are in the match for maybe an hour and under pressure for perhaps only five minutes. But the rest of the time the ball is in play, then you're in the game so you can't relax. It puts the muscles and joints through so much movement that negotiating day to day problems such as running for a bus then become easy.'

Complete beginners can quickly learn how to play and

within half an hour can maintain a rally. From there to the point where the beginner can play long enough to create a sweat is not far; when you start to play regularly, then you feel a new man. You feel better and, ergo, you work better. 'I met a chap at a party the other day', recalls Tony Swift (who is the SRA's Senior National Coach), 'who wasn't a good player by any means yet he was saying how he hadn't played for several months and consequently how awful he felt. Even at his standard he had noticed how much better he felt and worked. Oddly enough', Swift continued, 'although I still play a lot, because I am not match fit any more (Swift used to be ranked in the top dozen in England) I don't think that I work quite so well as I used to.'

A virtue of squash, allegedly, is that it helps to keep the weight down. A loss of '1,000 calories an hour' was one doctor's estimate. Yet how many players last an hour? Most play only half that time and then put back all they have lost by a couple of pints in the bar.

You *can* lose weight by playing squash – but only in conjunction with some other method of dieting. Squash alone is of very dubious merit. Even the great Hashim Khan had a paunch when he first arrived in Britain, despite hours spent on the often concrete-floored, usually hot, courts of Pakistan. When he first went to America an enthusiast wrote: 'A round-headed baldish man with a high-bridged nose and dark serious eyes, he was squat in build, standing about five feet four and weighing around 140 pounds. His legs were short and on the spindly side and, particularly since he was barrel-chested and had the suspicion of a pot belly, he seemed curiously top-heavy.' And that of a man who was, and remains, the best squash player the world has ever seen.

To sum up: play squash to get fit: play squash to stay healthy: play squash to enjoy yourself. And don't blame me if you can't get a court. Thousands of people are beginning to think the same way as you are.

John Hopkins is squash correspondent of The Sunday Times.

THE WOMEN'S GAME

Gillian Edwards

The exact date when women began to play squash is not known; what is fairly certain is that it was not long after the men. Very little was recorded about those early days, but by 1922 there was sufficient interest to hold the first women's championship.

Since then women's squash has come a long way, although Charles R. Read wrote in 1929: 'My advice is that a lady should leave a ball untried for, if to take it would entail a long run and quick return to position near the middle line.' The clothing worn at that time would probably have prevented 'a long run' anyway, for shorts were rarely seen as Mr Read observes: 'I have heard that in India ladies play this kind of game in "shorts", the male biped being excluded either as player or onlooker.' The reasons given for such masculine attire were that there was less chance of a fall in a corner, that any sort of skirt might 'mutilate' a low corner shot, and that skirts made players wider and so compelled them to take up more room on the court. He goes on to say that 'probably skirts must remain *en régle* in this country, since it is so common for men and women to find themselves in the same court'.

In 1932, when the women's championship had been in existence for 10 years, the Women's Squash Rackets Association was formed with the objective of promoting the game for women. This remains the Association's aim today. Chairman Ann Jackson feels that the WSRA is now sufficiently flexible to cope with rapidly changing demands, and able to lead the game's development. An example of this is the introduction of amateur coaching courses; there are now more than 150 elementary coaches who have qualified to teach the rudiments of the game. Another highly successful project, which is just beginning to reap dividends, is the county coaching scheme under which promising junior girls receive help. The best then go forward to the second stage of coaching at national level when there is a further selection process. Those players who reach the final stage are approaching junior international standard. At this stage they are 'mothered' by senior players, i.e. each junior is looked after by a senior. This scheme has been in progress for about four years, and the first British girls to emerge and make their impact on the squash world are Jane Courtney and Sue Cogswell.

With the surge of interest in the game in recent years the demands on the WSRA have increased considerably. The days of an honorary secretary who was expected to cope with everything ended in 1970, when Jean Wilson was appointed as the first paid official in the capacity of Secretary/Development Officer. Jean firmly believes that the overall standard of squash in Britain is improving and that the juniors are showing signs of the coaching and interest shown in them. Just 10 years ago all the top squash players in Britain were tennis girls – but now the players who have been taught squash from the beginning are coming to the forefront.

Although Jean is confident that the WSRA is reaching most girls who have any squash talent, she is concerned about the plight of those who receive coaching at school and then find that there is nowhere they can play. Apart from this she is satisfied that through the various coaching schemes, the network of tournaments, and the county organisations, the WSRA will discover those with potential.

For the last two seasons the WSRA has had a national coach, Jane Poynder. Her function is to train coaches, including school PE teachers, and encourage local authorities to introduce squash into schools.

The professional game for women is limited and is unlikely to develop along the lines of the men's, i.e. with sponsored tournaments. Women professionals are generally limited to coaching, although with the introduction of open tournaments in the 1973–74 season they were also allowed to participate in the inter-county matches and the home internationals.

All the principal squash-playing countries have squash associations for women, although in South Africa and New Zealand they are part of the men's organisation. The Australian Women's Squash Rackets Association is a separate body which came into being in the 1950s, with headquarters in Sydney. The Association runs on completely different lines from the British counterpart, a result of the vast distances in Australia which create an entirely different situation. Each state is autonomous and runs its own tournaments, conducts its own coaching schemes, and helps up-and-coming players. Thus the main function of the Australian WSRA is to promote overseas play with visits abroad, encourage visitors to Australia, run the Australian Championship, the inter-state championships, select the seeds for these events, and choose Australian teams.

Squash players from all the states only congregate once a year, at the Australian Championships which are held over two weeks. During the first week the individual championship takes place; then the inter-state championships are played in the second week, when the annual conference of the Australian WSRA also takes place.

The success of the Australian women's team during their visit to the United Kingdom last season speaks for itself so far as standard is concerned. Apart from Marion Jackman all the team were new internationals and there were several others back in Australia who were nearly as good. Not only that, Mrs Carol Murray, the Honorary Secretary of the Australian WSRA, says that the prospects for the future are extremely promising with a third of all women squash players taking part in competitive squash and yet another Australian squash boom taking off.

It is generally accepted that Australian standards are higher because their players show greater dedication and determination, and are prepared to train harder.

This difference in standards was apparent at the Langham Life Women's British Open Championship, played at Wembley. For the first time there was such a large entry that not all applications were accepted.

The strong Australian contingent provided seven of the 16 seeded players but there was never any doubt that Heather McKay would win the championship for the 14th consecutive year. The interest centred on whether the rest of the seeding had been correctly predicted.

There were no first round upsets although No. 4 seed Sue Cogswell struggled for her 7-9, 9-4, 9-3, 8-10, 9-3 win against Mrs Barniville of Dublin. The first seed went out in the second round with the defeat of Mrs Jane Courtney (No. 7) by Mrs Irene Hewitt, 9-5, 6-9, 9-7, 9-5. Mrs Hewitt went on to cause a further upset by defeating No. 10 seed Mrs Fran Marshall, 9-1, 9-5, 5-9, 9-1, in the next round. Two other wins against the seeding were Chris van Nierop's defeat of Teresa Lawes, who was placed one above her at No. 8, by 9-6, 9-5, 2-9, 9-2, and the win of Lyle Hubinger (No. 11) over Jean Wilson (No.6) by 9-6, 9-7, 9-0.

The quarter-finals saw the end of Sue Cogswell's challenge when she lost to Margaret Zachariah, 9-1, 9-5, 9-3, and Irene Hewitt's fine run of wins was ended by Marion Jackman who won 9-5, 9-2, 9-2. This meant that the semi-finals were contested by four Australians. The first semi-final was between Heather McKay and Margaret Zachariah, seeded No. 5, with the defending champion never allowing the challenger to show her earlier good form. Miss Zachariah collected only two points in a decisive win by Mrs McKay, the score being 9-1, 9-0, 9-1.

The other semi-final was an exciting 90-minute battle between second and third seeds Marion Jackman and Sue Newman. All except the fourth game, which Miss Newman appeared to let go, were closely fought and the difference between the contestants was marginal. Mrs Jackman's greater experience against the younger Miss Newman eventually told, and Mrs Jackman went through to the final 7-9, 9-4, 9-10, 9-1, 9-6.

The all-Australian final between Heather McKay and

Marion Jackman produced a masterly performance by Mrs McKay. After Mrs Jackman had gone into a surprise 3-0 lead, Mrs McKay began applying pressure and recovered to win 9-3. The second game score of 9-1 to Mrs McKay did not represent the close battle that took place, and although Mrs Jackman was hand-in several times she could not win two consecutive points to add to her score. In the third game it was much the same until Mrs McKay was 6-1 ahead. Then, her challenger, by an all-out effort, rallied to 5-7 before Mrs McKay took the two points needed to retain the championship.

Now that the game is spreading into Europe it is to be hoped that it will not be long before countries such as Holland and Sweden produce players good enough to take part in the championship. The future of the international game in North America seems uncertain, as although there are now some international-sized courts, the majority are built to the American dimensions. Whether the Americans will ever really take to the international game remains to be seen, but it seems a shame that a nation that has produced so many top sportswomen is not truly represented in squash.

RESULTS

FIRST ROUND

Mrs B. McKay (Aus) bt Mrs M. Rust 9-0, 9-0, 9-0
Miss C. Richards bt Mrs B. Diggens 2-9, 9-3, 9-3, 9-0
Mrs S. Murray (Aus) bt Miss S. Vesperman 9-2, 9-2, 9-5
Mrs S. Peach bt Mrs S. Lynas 9-6, 9-4, 9-3
Miss T. Lawes bt Miss K. Hall 9-2, 9-0, 9-1
Mrs A. Jee bt Miss D. McNeill 9-4, 9-0, 9-3
Miss C. Van Nierop (Aus) bt Mrs E. Popplewell 9-1, 9-4, 9-3
Mrs J. Ward bt Mrs S. Parker 9-2, 9-3, 9-0
Miss S. Cogswell bt Mrs H. Barniville 7-9, 9-4, 9-3, 8-10, 9-3
Miss D. Armstrong bt Miss L. Pyke 9-4, 9-6, 9-4
Mrs A. Chapman bt Mrs V. Corbett 9-4, 9-0, 9-6
Mrs J. Sheasby bt Miss J. Ledger 9-1, 9-7, 6-9, 9-6
Miss M. Zachariah (Aus) bt Miss A. Morris 9-2, 9-0, 9-2
Miss L. Moore bt Miss J. Poynder 6-9, 9-4, 9-3, 9-2
Miss T. Veltman bt Mrs C. Innocent 10-9, 9-4, 9-3
Miss C. Machin bt Mrs S. Warnes 9-2, 1-9, 9-6, 9-1
Mrs J. Reynolds w.o. Mrs M. James scr
Miss L. Hubinger (Aus) bt Mrs A. Manley 9-3, 9-3, 9-0
Mrs S. Dunford bt Miss V. Grisogono 9-4, 8-10, 9-6, 9-2
Miss J. Wilson bt Miss A. Price 9-0, 9-5, 9-2
Dr S. Pexman bt Mrs I. Sanderson 2-9, 6-9, 9-6, 9-4, 9-2
Miss K. Gardner bt Miss P. Lenehan 9-1, 9-0, 9-4
Mrs D. Murray bt Miss J. Ashton 6-9, 9-7, 9-6, 9-3
Miss S. Newman (Aus) bt Mrs D. Fuller 9-4, 9-3, 9-2
Mrs F. Corbett bt Miss S. Findlay 9-2, 7-9, 9-0, 9-0
Mrs G. Marshall bt Mrs J. Prichett 9-7, 9-1, 9-2
Mrs I. Hewitt bt Miss B. Carmichael 9-4, 9-0, 9-6
Mrs S. Courtney bt Mrs J. Cartwright 9-1, 9-0, 9-2

Mrs J. Wainwright bt Mrs R. Turner 9-6, 9-1, 9-0
Miss V. Bridgens (SA) bt Mrs J. Morrison 9-4, 9-7, 9-4
Mrs J. Maycock w.o. Mrs T. Lawrence scr
Mrs D. Jackman (Aus) bt Miss D. Allen (SA) 9-2, 9-1, 9-3

SECOND ROUND
Mrs McKay w.o. Miss Richards scr
Mrs Murray bt Mrs Peach 9-2, 9-4, 9-2
Miss Lawes bt Mrs Jee 9-4, 5-9, 9-1, 9-2
Miss Van Nierop bt Mrs Ward 9-0, 9-2, 9-1
Miss Cogswell bt Miss Armstrong 9-3, 9-3, 9-0
Mrs Chapman bt Mrs Sheasby 9-5, 9-1, 0-9, 9-3
Miss Zachariah bt Miss Moore 9-1, 9-1, 9-0
Miss Veltman bt Miss Machin 5-9, 9-2, 9-0, 9-7
Miss Hubinger bt Mrs Reynolds 9-2, 9-2, 9-2
Miss Wilson bt Mrs Dunford 9-1, 9-0, 9-4
Miss Gardner bt Dr Pexham 9-2, 9-4, 9-7
Miss Newman bt Mrs Murray 9-1, 9-1, 9-0
Mrs Marshall bt Mrs Corbett 9-5, 9-4, 9-2
Mrs Hewitt bt Mrs Courtney 9-5, 6-9, 9-7, 9-5
Miss Bridgens bt Mrs Wainright 9-4, 9-5, 2-9, 2-9, 9-0
Mrs Jackman bt Mrs Maycock 9-2, 9-1, 9-2

THIRD ROUND
Mrs McKay bt Mrs Murray 9-1, 9-0, 9-0
Miss Van Nierop bt Miss Lawes 9-6, 9-5, 2-9, 9-2
Miss Cogswell bt Mrs Chapman 10-8, 9-1, 9-3
Miss Zachariah bt Miss Veltman 4-9, 9-5, 9-2, 9-0
Miss Hubinger bt Miss Wilson 9-6, 9-7, 9-0
Miss Newman bt Miss Gardner 9-2, 9-1, 9-5
Mrs Hewitt bt Mrs Marshall 9-1, 9-5, 5-9, 9-1
Mrs Jackman bt Miss Bridgens 9-1, 9-2, 9-10, 9-1

FOURTH ROUND
Mrs McKay bt Miss Van Nierop 9-1, 9-2, 9-0
Miss Zachariah bt Miss Cogswell 9-1, 9-5, 9-3
Miss Newman bt Miss Hubinger 9-5, 9-1, 10-8
Mrs Jackman bt Mrs Hewitt 9-5, 9-2, 9-2

SEMI-FINALS
Mrs McKay bt Miss Zachariah 9-1, 9-0, 9-1
Mrs Jackman bt Miss Newman 7-9, 9-4, 9-10, 9-1, 9-6

FINAL
Mrs McKay bt Mrs Jackman 9-3, 9-1, 9-5

GREAT BRITAIN v AUSTRALIA 1975

The Australians arrived in London in February without their invincible spearhead, Heather McKay. This fact gave the British women a not unrealistic hope that they might win the series. But the hope was ill-founded, because Britain lost 3-0 – the host nation spent most of the time in a brave but losing struggle.

One exception was Jane Courtney's efficient and welcome win over Lyle Hubinger in the first test at Bournemouth, but the harsh facts were that the Australians were too fit, too powerful, and too consistent. The better technique and crisper striking of the ball by the visitors put Britain at an immediate disadvantage, and whenever there was a hint of danger the Australians were prepared to engage in exhausting rallies.

Britain led briefly, Jane Courtney taking advantage of a nervous and jittery start by Lyle Hubinger. She played aggressive and tidy squash, moving in to take the early ball and was 2-0 and 8-0 up before Lyle realised what was happening. Then the nearness of victory hit the British girl as well and she was thankful to scrape home 10-9 in that game.

Jean Wilson and Sue Cogswell both started off well early on in their respective matches against Sue Newman and Marion Jackman, but for different reasons neither could maintain control. Jean, trying to foil Sue Newman's tremendous power with a slower, cat-and-mouse game, was eventually forced into errors. Sue Cogswell, short of match play after her ankle injury, hit plenty of winners but unfortunately made many unforced mistakes. This played into the hands of Marion Jackman who specialises in a sound, risk-free game with boasts and drives.

The pattern of Australian domination continued in the second test at Brandon Hall, although Sue Cogswell, playing in front of her own Midlands supporters, did manage to take a game.

At No. 3 string for the last two matches, the Australians brought in Margaret Zachariah, a powerful, classical player. If Jane Courtney could repeat the control and aggression shown at Bournemouth then there were hopes of one win; but faced with a different style of play, she became flustered and inaccurate. Margaret pinned Jane behind her all the time with penetrating drives and then took advantage of the situation by playing the angle. Jane could not find any rhythm or consistency, despite grim determination and some valiant retrieving.

A bonus for the British team was the victory by Teresa Lawes over Chris van Nierop in the reserve match – played on a fast court and full of gruelling, hard-fought rallies. Teresa dug in and kept control, deservedly winning 9-5, 10-9, 10-8.

The series was now lost, but there was great determination on the part of the British side to put up a good performance at Wembley, in the first women's event to be staged at the new centre. There was a full gallery and plenty of patriotic support but it did nothing to inspire the British girls. Teresa Lawes came in at No. 3 for her first full international and was unlucky to face Margaret Zachariah in one of her most efficient moods. Teresa plays a similar sound type of game to Margaret but was lacking in pace, speed, and consistency.

WOMEN'S TEST SERIES

GREAT BRITAIN V AUSTRALIA
British names first

FIRST TEST
West Hants Club, Bournemouth, 12 February 1975
1 Miss S. Cogswell lost to Mrs M. Jackman 6-9, 1-9, 2-9
2 Miss J. Wilson lost to Miss S. Newman 8-10, 0-9, 4-9
3 Mrs S. Courtney bt Miss L. Hubinger 9-1, 9-2, 10-9
Reserve match Miss T. Lawes lost to Miss M Zachariah 10-9, 2-9, 1-9, 0-9
Australia won 2-1

SECOND TEST *(sponsored by Falcon Inns Limited)*
Brandon Hall, Coventry, 19 February 1975
1 Miss S. Cogswell lost to Mrs M. Jackman 7-9, 7-9, 9-7, 2-9
2 Miss J. Wilson lost to Miss S. Newman 4-9, 2-9, 6-9
3 Mrs S. Courtney lost to Miss M. Zachariah 6-9, 3-9, 3-9
Reserve match Miss T. Lawes lost to Miss M. Zachariah 9-5, 10-9, 10-8
Australia won 3-0

THIRD TEST
Wembley, 26 February 1975
1 Miss S. Cogswell lost to Mrs M. Jackman 4-9, 2-9, 5-9
2 Miss J. Wilson lost to Miss S. Newman 8-10, 4-9, 3-9
3 Miss T. Lawes lost to Miss M. Zachariah 3-9, 4-9, 2-9
Reserve match Mrs S. Courtney lost to Miss L. Hubinger 6-9, 7-9, 9-4, 1-9
Australia won 3-0

SOME FEMALE FACES

VAL BRIDGENS

South African Val Bridgens, from Port Elizabeth, took up squash to fill in the spare time she had after giving up training two hours a day for swimming. That was in March 1970. By the end of the season, in September, she was taking the sport seriously and had been selected as reserve for Eastern Province. She now plays No. 1 for that province, has been its champion for the past four years and the South African Under 23 Champion for the last three.

Due to distance problems, Val plays most of her squash in her own province, except for the South African championships. Last year in this event she reached the quarter-finals where she was beaten by eventual finalist Gay Erskine.

Val's ultimate aim is to win selection for South Africa; after all she now has the experience of two visits to Britain behind her.

DIANNE ALLAN

Dianne Allan, born in Umtati, Rhodesia, in April 1948, was Rhodesian tennis champion for three years before taking up squash quite by chance in 1972. She immediately decided that squash presented a greater challenge to her and gave up tennis to concentrate on her new sport.

This dedication paid dividends within six months with Dianne playing for Rhodesia in the Southern African Inter-Provincial tournament—a major tournament that Rhodesia has won for the past three years. Dianne, ranked No.2 in Rhodesia, behind Gay Erskine, was sent to England last season by the Squash Rackets Association of South Africa, to which the Rhodesian association is affiliated. This has helped towards fulfilling her ambition to improve and learn more about the game of squash.

SUE COGSWELL

Sue Cogswell's introduction to squash came in 1971, but before this she had reached county standard in tennis, representing Warwickshire. This meant that when Sue decided to concentrate her talents on squash she had to work much harder to gain recognition. Most of her contemporaries had come up through the county coaching scheme and established themselves as juniors while Sue was busy making headway in the world of tennis.

After Sue moved to London to train as a physiotherapist she played in the Greater London Cup in October 1971, which pushed her into a far more competitive squash environment. Sue soon realised that she would have to choose between tennis and squash if she was to reach a high standard in either.

The decision made to concentrate on squash, she improved rapidly and was selected for England in the home international against Ireland in March 1972. Important as this was, Sue regards her defeat of Fran Marshall in the quarter-finals of the Welsh Open in November 1972 as the start of her rise in the squash world. From then on she made rapid progress and in February 1973 gained full international honours for Great Britain against New Zealand. The following summer she was one of the players to visit South Africa on a WSRA sponsored tour and returned a much improved player.

This progress continued through the 1973–74 season and by the end of it she was the British No. 1, having reached the final of the women's championships in which she was beaten by Heather McKay 9-2, 9-1, 9-1. Sue toured South Africa again in the summer of 1974, but the 1974–75 British season did not live up to expectations as she sustained an ankle injury which kept her out of competitive squash for some weeks and left her short of match practice. However, Sue was seeded No. 4 for the Langham Life Women's British Open Championships, reaching the quarter-finals where she was defeated by Australian Margaret Zachariah.

Just before the championships Sue qualified as a physiotherapist and has now moved back to Birmingham to work. She feels that, Heather McKay excepted, women's world squash is wide open, and is determined to give herself a set period in which to work at the sport.

'After all', says Sue, 'if I don't try I shall always wonder how far I *could* have gone.'

JEAN WILSON

Jean Wilson started playing squash at the age of 17 at the Manchester Northern Club, in a typically British way – she had gone there to play tennis, but because of rain played squash instead. Fortunately for Jean, she received much encouragement from two members of the club, ex-international Mrs Dorothy Cooper and Mrs Sadie Youatt.

Due to Jean's greater interest in tennis (she played for Lancashire for several years) and studies, it was not until the beginning of the 1969–70 season that she decided to take squash seriously. A few months later she came to London to take up the post of secretary to the Women's Squash Rackets Association, which entailed the promotion of squash in Britain and involved Jean in travelling throughout the country.

Jean gained full international status in 1971 when she was selected to play at No. 3 in the British team against Australia. That summer she toured South Africa with Jane Courtney and Theo Veltman, then the following year she was one of the British team to visit Australia and New Zealand, playing at No. 2, and in 1973 she toured South Africa again.

In the 1974–75 season Jean captained the British team against the visiting Australians. This was also her last season in British squash as she gave up her post with the WSRA in order to marry South African Chris Grainger in May. She now lives in Johannesburg.

HEATHER McKAY

Heather McKay is the first to admit that she doesn't really know why she is so much better at squash than all the other women players in the world. She feels that it is a combination of things, and no one individual aspect of her game or physique. Whatever it is, Heather has remained unbeaten, and seemingly unbeatable, since 1962.

Heather first played squash in 1959, to keep fit for hockey, but within 12 months she had decided to concentrate on her new sport. Her first success was in April 1960, when she won the New South Wales Country junior and senior women's singles. It was also the occasion on which she met Vin Napier for the first time. He was then the President of the Australian men's squash association, and it was largely due to his encouragement that Heather entered the New South Wales championships. Here she won the junior singles and did enough to ensure selection for New South Wales in the inter-state team. Shortly after, Heather had to play in the elimination round of the Australian Championship – and went on to win it for the first time. The following year, 1961, she added the New South Wales and Victorian titles; and went on winning them until she turned professional.

Heather McKay – her superiority in matches is the result of self-discipline and concentration.

Heather's first visit to Britain was in 1962 when she was sent by the Australian Women's Squash Association to compete in the British Women's Championship, which she won by beating Fran Marshall in the final. In 1975 she has won the championship for the 14th time, and in all those years she has only ever dropped one game – in 1964, to Anna Craven-Smith in the semi-finals. Heather McKay's remarkable record and services to the sport of squash rackets were recognised when she was awarded the MBE in the 1969 New Year Honours List.

Squash has taken Heather to many parts of the world, including New Zealand, South Africa, Great Britain, North America, Sweden, Denmark, and Germany, and she would like to see the international game become established throughout the world, particularly in the United States and Japan.

The difference in standard between Heather and other women players appears as big as ever, but she says that her superiority in matches is the result of self-dicipline and concentration. Off court, Heather trains five times a week by running and doing exercises.

Having fulfilled all her ambitions in competitive squash, Heather turned professional in January 1974 and has held coaching clinics in the UK and Australia. Her particular aim, so far as coaching is concerned, is to coach junior girls to become top class players.

Marion Jackman – well known for her speed around the court.

MARION JACKMAN

Marion Jackman is only too happy to step into the shoes of Heather McKay as Australia's No. 1 woman amateur player. This has been her ultimate aim after achieving the ambition of winning the Australian championship.

She belongs to the same club in Brisbane as Heather, but they captain different teams in the same league and still play each other competitively on occasions. Marion has the distinction of having taken more games than anyone else from the champion but admits that the gulf between them is still as wide as ever. 'Heather', she says, 'is now working harder at her game than before and is going into the placement of the ball scientifically.'

Marion has played top squash for over 10 years, first playing for her state, Queensland, in 1963, and for Australia two years later. She has been Queensland champion for 11 years in succession – a record for the state. A beautiful shot-player, Marion is nick-named 'fairy feet' because of her fine strokes, her flexibility, and speed around the court. Invariably her feet are correctly placed and her backhand boast is a delight to watch.

On her visit to Britain in 1975 she was accompanied by her husband David who plays No. 4 for Queensland. She has considered turning professional but is in no hurry to make up her mind.

JENNY IRVING

Jenny, a tall, strong squash player, is regarded as one of the veterans of women's squash. She gave up tennis 16 years ago and started to play squash under the coaching of Bryan Boyce, Geoff Hunt's coach in Melbourne. Within a year she was playing for Victoria. In 1967 she moved to Sydney, New South Wales, and represented that state until 1970. A year later the Irving family transferred to Perth, and she played for Western Australia in 1972. A final move to Brisbane, Queensland, brought Jenny the distinction of having represented five states.

Like her colleagues, Jenny has suffered through the domination of Heather McKay and has been runner-up in many state championships as well as the Australian championship. She has represented Australia since 1965, and on the 1971 tour to Britain earned the nickname of 'flash' as she was always last and slowest to get ready.

Her determination, together with her aggressive power game is probably the outstanding feature of her technique. Aub Amos, one of Queensland's top professional coaches, comments: 'She never knows when to give up. When she is down and out and exhausted in the back corner she somehow comes back and that's when Jenny plays her best squash.' She is also admired for her good sportsmanship both on and off the court.

Jenny Irving – determination and aggressive power are outstanding features of her game.

THE JUNIOR GAME

Tony Swift

Junior squash in England has taken several large strides forward – the growth of the game at this level has been most encouraging. However, it may be appropriate to define the status of 'junior' before discussing recent developments. Until the start of the 1974–75 season, a junior was a player under the age of 19 on 1 January. This was fine in England, but not so good for junior players overseas having different seasons. The International Squash Rackets Federation decided that a suitable compromise, and one that has been adopted by the Squash Rackets Association, is to define a junior as being a player under the age of 19 on the first day of the tournament in question. This decision has created problems on the home front but seems to be a fair one internationally.

Three years ago the most important junior tournament was the Drysdale Cup, organised and run by the RAC. It was regarded by most as the junior 'Open' and has been running for 50 years. Many famous names appear on the roll of honour, including Nigel Broomfield, Jeremy Lyon, Mike Oddy, Mike Corby, Bryan Patterson, Stuart Courtney, John Richardson, and Peter Verow, all of whom have represented their country, and (in 1971) a youngster from Pakistan, the current amateur champion, Mohibullah Khan. The Bath Club run an equivalent championship for players under 16 and these, with an increasing number of other tournaments, have been the junior fixture list.

One of the most pressing problems that I had to face when appointed in 1972 was what happened to a junior, whether or not he won a tournament, once he reached his age limit. It is a big step from being a good junior to becoming a good senior and I felt that too many youngsters were being lost because they could not make the transition on their own. Unless they had tremendous determination or outstanding skill they were lost to the squash world. To help bridge the gap, I formed a national junior squad. The incentives thus created have reaped the reward for which I was looking. After three years the boys in the current squad are classes above other players of their own age, and Philip Kenyon, current holder of

Philip Kenyon has dominated the British junior scene for several years. He retained his British junior title and is seen here with his trophy and Doug Crocker, director of the tournament sponsors, Falcon Inns. (Photo by Maurice Mead)

the British junior title and the Drysdale Cup, has already toured South Africa with the Great Britain 'senior' team.

There are signs that other players have the potential to become as good if not better than Philip, but probably the most encouraging aspect to emerge is the squad's level of dedication and fitness. This will stand them all in good stead when they reach the age limit and many of them already hold their own in senior circles.

Next came a junior international festival, a reward for top boys in the squad as well as an encouragement to other countries to develop squash at this level. The festival has been running for three years, with teams from Wales and Scotland competing annually. It has been noticeable that both these sides have benefited from the development which has taken place as a direct result of the festival. It is regrettable that a junior team from Ireland have yet to participate, but should the festival find its way to Dublin there must be a good chance that the last member of the home countries would enter a team.

In its first year, the festival welcomed a team from Sweden where the greatest development in junior squash that I have witnessed from any country, including England, has taken place over the last five years. This is due to sponsorship and, I believe, to government backing. In England growth has tended to be limited to the extent of sponsorship available, of which the sum total is probably less than 25 per cent of what has been achieved in Sweden.

Sweden are a country new to squash and sensibly their policy has been to develop the game at the junior level. Already the results are being felt – for in April of this year Sweden beat a rather surprised Irish team. The Irish would do well to learn from their victors.

Last year a team from South Africa competed in the festival and while it was not a national side, the boys had competed in the final stages of the South African Junior Championships. It would appear from their results that the junior game in South Africa still has some way to go.

The England juniors won both festivals easily and remained unbeaten. In 1975, in Scotland, a junior side from Egypt arrived at the last minute and finished as runners-up to England, after close matches with both Wales and the host nation. It was encouraging to see another team although disappointing that another seven countries who had been invited from Europe, the Middle and Far East were unable to compete. Pakistan presumably could not afford to send a team because they already have a squad of 16, including youngsters, who train daily. It is frightening to hear Mohibullah and Zaman talking of younger brothers both of whom show more potential than their famous elders.

They start 'em young at Gresham's School, Norwich. From the left, Martin Cuff, aged 8, Christy Willstrop 11, John Cordeaux 14, Nicholas Chesworth 14, Duncan Bruce-Lockhart 13, and Gawain Briars 17. (Photo by A. Griffee)

So the England juniors are holding their own and improving with each year; but the development pyramid must broaden its base if it is to be successful. Falcon Inns assisted in 1974–75 by sponsoring nine area junior tournaments – a step in the right direction. With time it is hoped that area junior squads can be formed from which the national squad will be chosen. So far I have been discussing the under 19 age-group, but many tournaments also run under 16 and under 14 age-groups with considerable success, not only in terms of quantity but also quality.

In two and a half years I have now conducted over 20 tours throughout the country and some of my lasting impressions have been of boys of 12 who are capable of setting up practices better than many senior county players. One boy of 12 I shall always remember who when asked how long he had been playing, replied: 'Eight years, sir.'

It was with considerable delight that a British Under 14 championship was inaugurated this year, thanks to the sponsorship of Darbrook. And what an eye-opener this tournament turned out to be; to say that the standard of play was high was an understatement. Techniques and tactics were already well developed in these young players who showed both discipline and determination. There were some excellent matches and at least 10 of the 35 competitors showed such potential that it makes an under 15 national squad a priority, to be the breeding ground for the under 19s.

To talk of the junior development scheme in England is to ignore the keen following that exists at county level. Here are a band of juniors who will never reach the heights, but who are as enthusiastic as those at the top. Many of them have shown considerable skill already in obtaining the junior proficiency certificate at one of three levels.

Tony Swift is Senior National Coach.

RESULTS

FALCON INNS BRITISH JUNIOR UNDER 19 CHAMPIONSHIP
P. Kenyon bt J. Le Lievre 9-5, 9-1, 9-3

DARBROOK BRITISH UNDER 14 CHAMPIONSHIP
D. Thomas bt J. Cook 9-1, 9-5, 9-1

THE FUTURE OF SQUASH

Alan Jenkins

Since the first amateur championship was held in 1906, the squash rackets industry has experienced some tremendous changes. The 1930s saw the first boom in court building, which came to a halt in 1939 before squash had become properly established. Post-war recovery restrained further development and it was not until the early 1960s that the sport took off once more.

In the nine years to 1972, courts affiliated to the Squash Rackets Association doubled, increasing at an annual rate of eight per cent. Thus there were then some 343,000 squash players in England, using around 2,300 courts. Since 1972 there is every reason to believe that the rate at which new courts have been opening is higher than eight per cent.

Racket sales – another indicator – of the three largest manufacturers in Britain rose annually by 18 per cent between 1962 and 1970. But with new companies entering the market from 1967 onwards and an increasing number of rackets being imported, even this high rate of change is understated. The backcloth against which expansion and growth should be viewed is an economy which has seen a series of dramatic upheavals.

In spite of the expansion, many clubs still have waiting lists of members wishing to join and those players who do have access to a court cannot always play for the time that they would like. The new Wembley Squash Centre, which opened in the autumn of 1974, gives some indication of the depth of demand: within a couple of months all 15 courts of this commercially-run complex were working almost to capacity. A newspaper article commented: 'you'll not get an evening court for tomorrow week unless you're in the telephone queue soon after breakfast'.

With commercial enterprises such as Bass-Charrington, J. Lyons, and Wates the builders opening their first centres, local authorities building sports centres, schools and 'member clubs' putting up courts, the growth of squash seems assured.

In the future, the big sector will be local authority centres. The Sports Council programme originally aimed at 850 establishments and an extra 2,500 squash courts by 1981. However, this was on the basis of two or three courts per centre, a norm which is often exceeded nowadays – few centres open with less than four courts. Alton Sports Centre in Hampshire, which opened in March 1975, has six glass-backed courts, and squash is one of the main features of the complex.

There are three important aspects of this kind of facility. Firstly, it brings squash within reach of a wider section of the population who hitherto had little or no opportunity of playing. Secondly, becoming a club member is not a pre-condition to participation as it has been in the past. As yet only the Wembley Squash Centre, among the commercial centres, has adopted the 'no membership' philosophy. In Australia, of course, there are many such centres. Thirdly, an economic price for playing is charged at local authority centres. Squash is probably the only sport that makes a profit and contributes substantially to total revenue. In essence it subsidises other activities (swimming, while popular, tends to be heavily subsidised by the rates).

New impetus to recreation and leisure provision has come from local government with centres that offer a combination of leisure facilities. This centre at Herringthorpe, Rotherham, in Yorkshire, contains squash courts, heated swimming pool, restaurant, and bar. (Photo courtesy of Rotherham Metropolitan Borough Council)

This last aspect is important. With centres experiencing a financial squeeze, managers look to their profitable facilities to relieve the pressure. Therefore, in development plans, it will be those sports able to provide a good income that will be given high priority.

With all this optimism, is there not a risk of too many courts being built? Unfortunately, it is impossible to estimate how many courts we need. One reason for this is that so many people have had little or no experience of the game. As a sport it has had little promotion, with reporting confined to a few newspapers and a little radio or television coverage – the first national television showing of squash in Britain was in February 1974.

However, a comparison can be made with New Zealand, where squash has been more widely developed. There they have one court for every 10,700 people: in England the ratio is one to every 16,000. The distribution, however, is patchy. In Christchurch (NZ) for example, in addition to their 42 squash courts they also have 20 golf clubs, plus many swimming, riding, and ski-ing establishments – as well as rugby, cricket, and football pitches. What town in Britain today with a population of 300,000 can boast such an abundance of sports facilities?

Radical changes over the past few years in central and local government will give new impetus to recreation and leisure provision. New departments are being set up based on a philosophy of combining *all* leisure activities within a social context. The outcome could be a more flexible approach to leisure provision. Durham and Teesside in the late 1960s was one of the first to combine the 'arts' with 'sport'.

But perhaps one of the most adventurous centres to open is at Cannon Hill Park, Birmingham – the Midlands Art Centre. There the range of activities covers sculpture, woodwork, music, squash, badminton, rock-climbing, a puppet theatre, films, painting, pottery, and a 'live' theatre where the aspiring actor or actress can learn the ropes as well as watch the professionals. The centre encourages children to work and play alongside their parents with emphasis on family participation and, if necessary, 'foster' parents are provided.

Emphasis on the social aspect of leisure encourages a variety of facilities: St Michael's Church in Welling, Kent, is building squash courts as part of a community centre; Cunard-Trafalgar Hotels opened a complex which included swimming, tennis, and squash; a successful week's residential sports holiday for families was provided through the Yorkshire and Humberside Sports Council. The concept of neighbourhood centres was one of the basic tenets of a special report by Michael Dixey (Local Recreation Centres). The existence of 'round the corner' facilities would encourage social communication between both families and

The advent of the glass back-wall and the research done by the Pilkington Glass Company in this respect has given squash a new dimension. (Photo courtesy of Pilkington)

individuals. Unfortunately, to recognise fully this 'socialising' aspect implies fun and enjoyment, which militates against the local authority concept of 'social need' – the rates are not levied for enjoyment.

However, even this attitude is changing amongst local authorities. (Bletchley Leisure Centre, for example, has a 'fun pool' which is kidney-shaped, and it has a definite South Sea Island atmosphere.) But it will take time before entrenched positions are abandoned. Change and flexibility is probably the catch-phrase for the next few years, both within the leisure industry as a whole and squash in particular.

Undoubtedly, squash will increasingly take the lead and become the cornerstone of any new leisure development, but it still has some way to go before it becomes one of the country's leading sports.

(Based on 'The case for squash: its growth, development and prospects' by Alan Jenkins: all copyright is reserved.)

PLAY THE JAHAN WAY

Hiddy Jahan

Hiddy Jahan is a professional from Pakistan currently enjoying a world ranking of number four. His prowess as a stroke-player is recognised throughout the world by all those who have watched him or played against him. For the first time he gives his instructions for successful stroke play and his views on tactics.

Squash has been likened to physical chess, which is a fairly accurate analogy. The player who can control the placement of the ball better, and who has the fitness and stamina to continue to do so, will emerge the winner from this two-man war.

Like gaining control of the net in tennis, the control of the centre of the squash court affords dominance of the game. All shots and movement revolve around the notion of gaining possession of the sacred centre court.

In general terms, all shots are placed to bounce as far away as possible from the centre in order to make your opponent run into the corners. Meanwhile, you can step into the middle and dominate; and should your opponent put the ball into a corner you are well placed to retrieve it. Starting from the centre minimises your movement. After every shot move back towards it, in preparation for the next placement from your opponent's racket.

That is the basis of the physical chess idea, although tactics go deeper – into the speed of the ball, into exposing technical flaws in an opponent's game, and a myriad of mental ploys all aimed at victory.

There are two ideas which cannot be overlooked at any stage. 'Watch the ball at all times' has been said often enough, but it really is a vital thing to remember even when you are in front of your opponent.

The grip on the racket is also very simple, but important in the sound formation of strokes. Take the shaft of the racket in the left hand and grasp it by the handle with the right, as though you are shaking hands with it. Now wrap your fingers around the handle. You should have formed a 'V' between your thumb and forefinger. The thumb does not run along the top of the handle, but curls round the opposite side, to meet the fingers. The heel of your hand should rest at the base of the grip.

This is the natural grip for most people, although there

have been some notable players who have adopted different versions, including Hashim Khan, the legendary seven times winner of the British Open.

Now, with these notions in your head you are ready to take the court to learn stroke production.

Forehand drive: the racket makes impact outside the front foot.

FOREHAND STRAIGHT DRIVE

The straight drive is the basic stroke in squash, the foundation for strategy, or tactics. The purpose of the shot is to hit the ball into the back corner so as to make it bounce for the second time as near to the back wall as possible. This is the 'length' shot which, when played accurately, forces your opponent on to the defensive – creating opportunities for your next stroke.

I start with my body facing towards the side wall, always remembering to keep tracking the ball with my eyes. My swing starts very early as soon as I recognise that the ball is coming on to my forehand flank. I take my racket up behind my head, not forgetting to keep my wrist at an angle of 90° to my forearm – this position being called 'cocked'.

On the down swing I transfer my weight on to my leading foot and make contact with the ball at a point directly in front of this foot. My racket face is now directly in line with my leading foot and square on to the ball. So the result of the shot must be one which rebounds straight up the side wall – the intended course.

The follow-through is important to give rhythm to the shot. The racket head swings high behind my head making an arc of over 180°, although at no stage being a dangerous obstruction to my opponent. (The strike action has often been likened to skimming a stone across water.) May I remind you to bend your knees and be light on your feet, on your toes!

BACKHAND STRAIGHT DRIVE

The thinking behind the backhand drive down the side wall, and the actual production of the stroke, are theoretically the same as for the forehand shot. Once again I start with my torso towards the side wall; as I take my backswing to its end point, I swivel away from the front wall although still keep my head turned to watch the ball. As the racket swings down to meet the ball, so the torso uncoils towards the front wall, the racket finally making impact once again outside the front foot. My weight distribution at this point of the stroke is firmly over the leading foot and it is the uncoiling of the torso and shifting of the weight on to the front foot that generates power.

It is important always to keep a comfortable distance away from the ball. You can check this by making sure your shoulder is down at the point of impact, ensuring that the follow-through is not wild and dangerous.

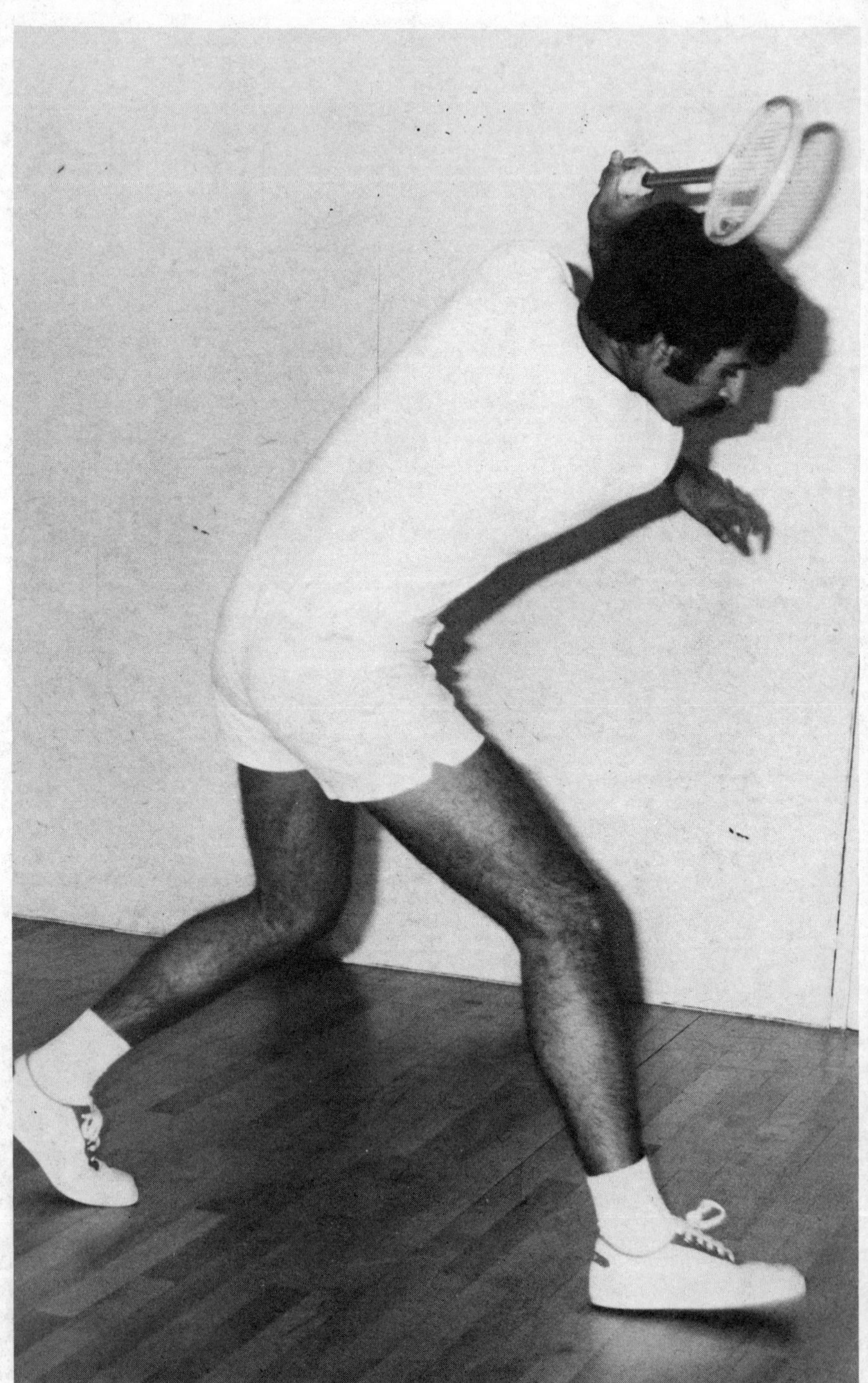

Backhand straight drive: swivel away from the front wall and keep the head turned to watch the ball.

Forehand drop: address the shot with feet sufficiently spread to be well balanced.

Throughout the stroke the cocked wrist is essential for control of the ball. By keeping the racket held firmly in this position you will be less prone to error.

Backhand drop (crosscourt): twist the wrist violently at the moment of impact.

FOREHAND DROP SHOT

Having created the opportunity with sound length to play an outright winner, the drop shot is the most delicate kill shot of all. No player can afford to be without an accurate, even if unspectacular, drop shot in his repertoire. When moving into the front corners of the court to approach the short ball, make sure that you address the shot with your feet spread sufficiently to be well balanced. Bend your back and get down to the ball. It is more than likely that the shot will be bouncing on a low trajectory so you may even have to stretch – but keep your balance, and bend your knees and back. Don't simply lower the racket head, for the consequences are usually fatal.

With my eyes glued to the ball, I always try to keep the racket face open. The point of impact should once again be in line with the direction of the front foot. If you have to over-stretch to make contact with the ball don't try to play an outright winner, rather play for safety with a lob.

Most drop shots are completed with a short follow-through which is accompanied by the return to the upright position and movement away from the placement of the ball. This will not only prepare you for your next shot, but also help you to give access to your opponent should he be able to return the ball.

BACKHAND DROP SHOT (AND CROSSCOURT)

The backhand drop shot is constructed on the same principles as the forehand, but, if anything, they need to be followed even more closely. If the ball does not die quietly on the first or second bounce in the nick – the right angle join of the floor and side wall – then a tight shot that clings to the side wall can be just as effective.

I try to take the pace off the ball by opening my racket face. This means I turn my wrist towards my body, like slicing the ball in tennis, and expose a greater angle of the racket face towards the ceiling and less towards the ball. A margin for error is creeping in here, but it does ensure that the ball will fly upwards, hopefully over the tin, once it has left the strings.

Another important aspect of the backhand drop is to play the ball away from the body. It is all very well to shield the ball with your body and so deceive your opponent, but too often players strike the ball off their chests; and without control, deception is irrelevant.

To play the crosscourt shot from either flank I believe in, and use, only wristwork. Employing the same footwork and the same short backswing, I suddenly twist my wrist violently at the moment of impact to change the direction

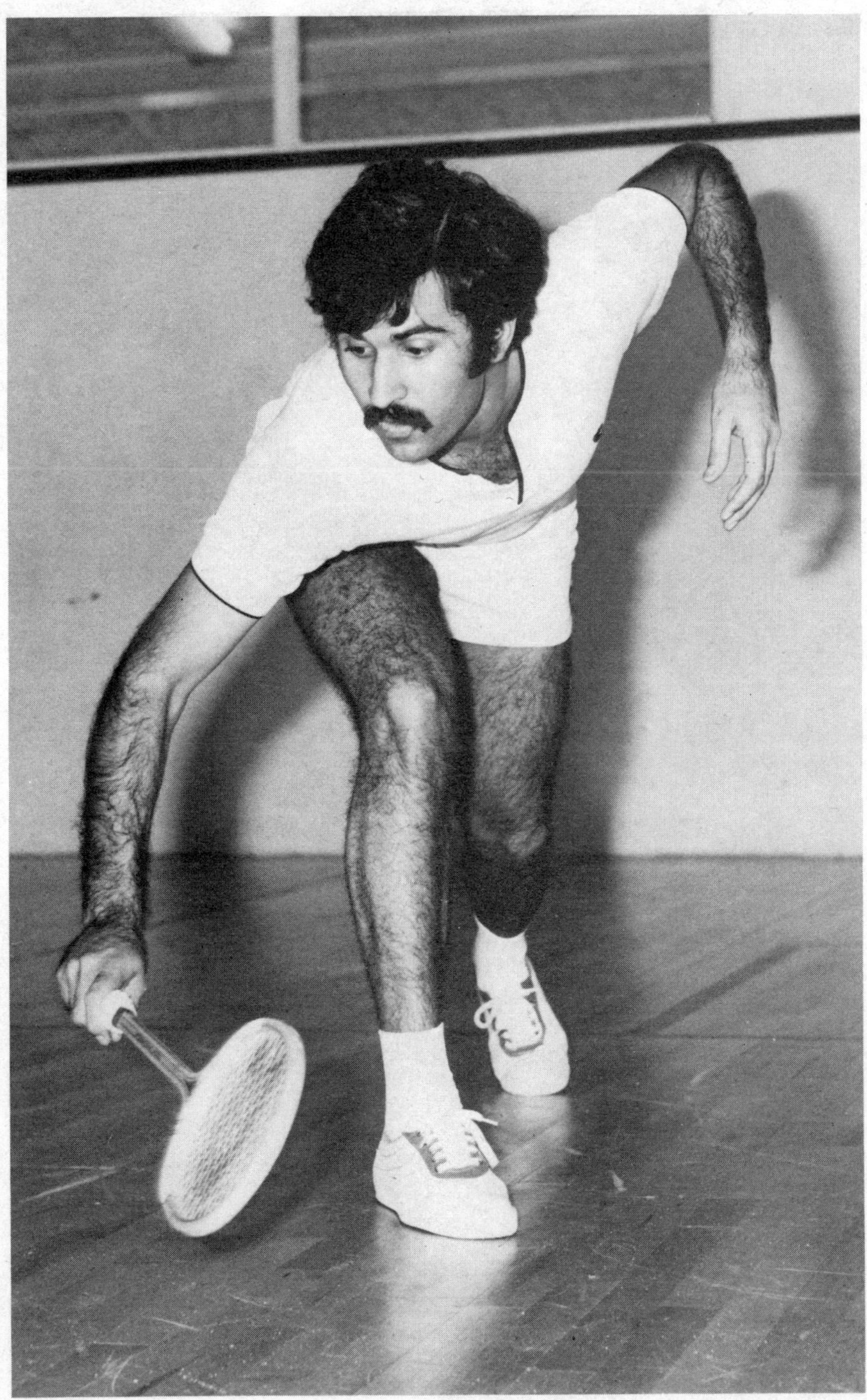

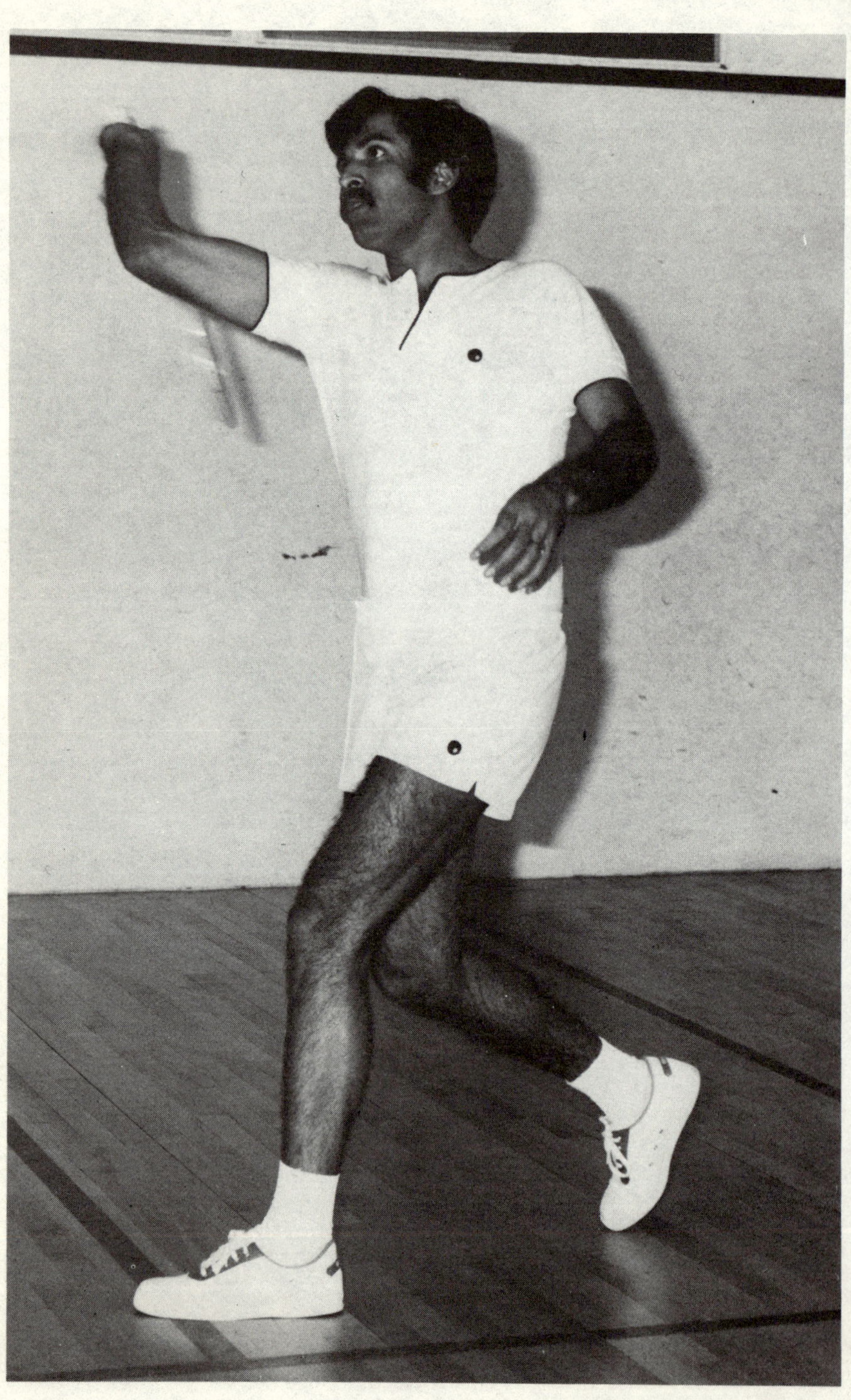

Left *The volley: contact between racket and ball is made in front of the leading foot.*

Below *The lob: open the racket face and lift the ball high on to the front wall.*

of the racket face and so send the ball sharply across the front wall, skidding into the opposite side wall – perhaps even into the nick. The element of surprise contributes largely to the success of the stroke, but the wrist needs training and the shot itself enormous amounts of practice.

THE VOLLEY

Volleying the ball is one of the most aggressive shots in squash. By taking the ball out of the air you can unsettle your opponent into rushing his or her next shot, off balance; or if you are in a favourable position the volley

can be used effectively to kill the ball short into the front corners of the court.

The crosscourt drive: twist the body across the front wall in an exaggerated fashion.

The basic technique applies both to a length shot and a short kill, the difference in the effect being a product of wristwork again and hours of dedicated practice. The major problem in the volley is the large margin of error which creeps into the strokes of even the best ground-stroke players.

It is vital that the upper torso be sufficiently equipped in muscle development to play the ball properly. The muscles in the upper arm, not only the famous biceps, but the group behind the arm, the triceps, need strength to give a firm, unwavering backswing with the racket head well in control by the wrist held at the cocked position.

The feet and position of the body resemble that of the classic ground stroke – only the arc of the swing is elevated. Once again contact is made between racket and ball in front of the leading foot. Sound footwork will be of great benefit to the accuracy and power of the volley, so make sure you get into position correctly before commencing the backswing, and liven up your muscles to cope with the aerial arc.

THE LOB

With the emergence of power-pressure tactics being used by the top players to take the titles in recent years, and thus reliance on the volley as a major source of points, the lob has been regarded as a shot which you play only when forced, and never something you would elect to play strategically. This is really an injustice to a shot requiring great skill, which when used correctly can have great effect.

The lob is a gentle shot lofted through the heights of the court, which draws opponents into the rear corners. A loose lob becomes fodder for the sound volleyer of the ball, so height and width – ability to traverse the length of the court whilst remaining outside striking distance from its centre – are of paramount importance.

The stroke is of orthodox character in preparation whether struck from the front or rear of the court. With an ample, and early, backswing, open the racket face and lift the ball high on to the front wall. A combination of strength behind the shot and placement on to the front wall will determine whether you achieve good length, or disaster. In an effort to keep the ball wide of the centre of the court, I try to make the ball hit the side wall at the back corner in much the same manner as the lob serve.

As a tactical device the lob can be used not only to force your opponent into a defensive area of the court, but to stall for time and gain a breather, or regain the centre of the court. A change of pace in a thrashing match can put your opponent off, and may induce him or her to make an error.

The serve: position the body at an angle to the front wall so that impact is made outside the leading foot.

THE CROSSCOURT DRIVE

The crosscourt drive is my favourite shot. Whether I aim to attack directly, or to begin a rally with the stroke, I use broadly the same principles. My own approach to the shot differs from the general consensus of opinion in one crucial factor. Whereas orthodoxy and I agree on backswing, swing, and follow-through, which are all the same as for the straight drive, we have a divergence of opinion on how best to turn the ball across the court from the normal swing. General opinion says that the point of impact should be in front of the leading foot, i.e. a little later in the arc of the swing where the racket face is turning with the swing in the crosscourt direction. This is tantamount to taking the ball a fraction earlier, although my method is built upon surprise and is not quite so simple.

On the downswing of the shot before making contact with the ball, you must suddenly twist the torso towards the front wall in an exaggerated fashion compared with the flow of movement in the straight drive, As the body snaps around, the wrist turns sharply inwards without loosing the cocked formation and so changes the direction of the racket head which imparts this to the progress of the ball. The point of impact however, remains the same as for a straight drive. I connect with the ball in line with the leading foot: it is only the last minute turn of the torso and wrist that does the work.

The backhand requires less effort from the body, but in turn demands more strength of the wrist. Irrespective of whether you are aiming for a length shot or a stunning, powerful, short shot the idea is the same – just make sure that the ball is wide of the centre court.

THE SERVE

The service is arguably the most important shot in squash. After all, it is the only one that you never have to run after, and to that extent it should be the easiest to execute. Given the opportunity to influence the game unhindered by pressure of any kind, the serve should be taken seriously each and every time. Double faults are a crime. Never give your opponent a chance to serve unless he has earned it.

The serve can be a most damaging shot in club level squash, especially against opponents who have not learnt their boast lessons properly. In international squash, a service ace is a rarity, usually caused by the ball accidently hitting the nick. But the level at which you are playing does not matter; the serve's importance can never be underestimated. Everyone must consider the shot carefully before playing it; have a definite purpose in mind when you step into the service box.

Whether you are serving for an ace, or against a player thoroughly competent in service return, the aim should be the same for the basic service. The two serves, the lob, and

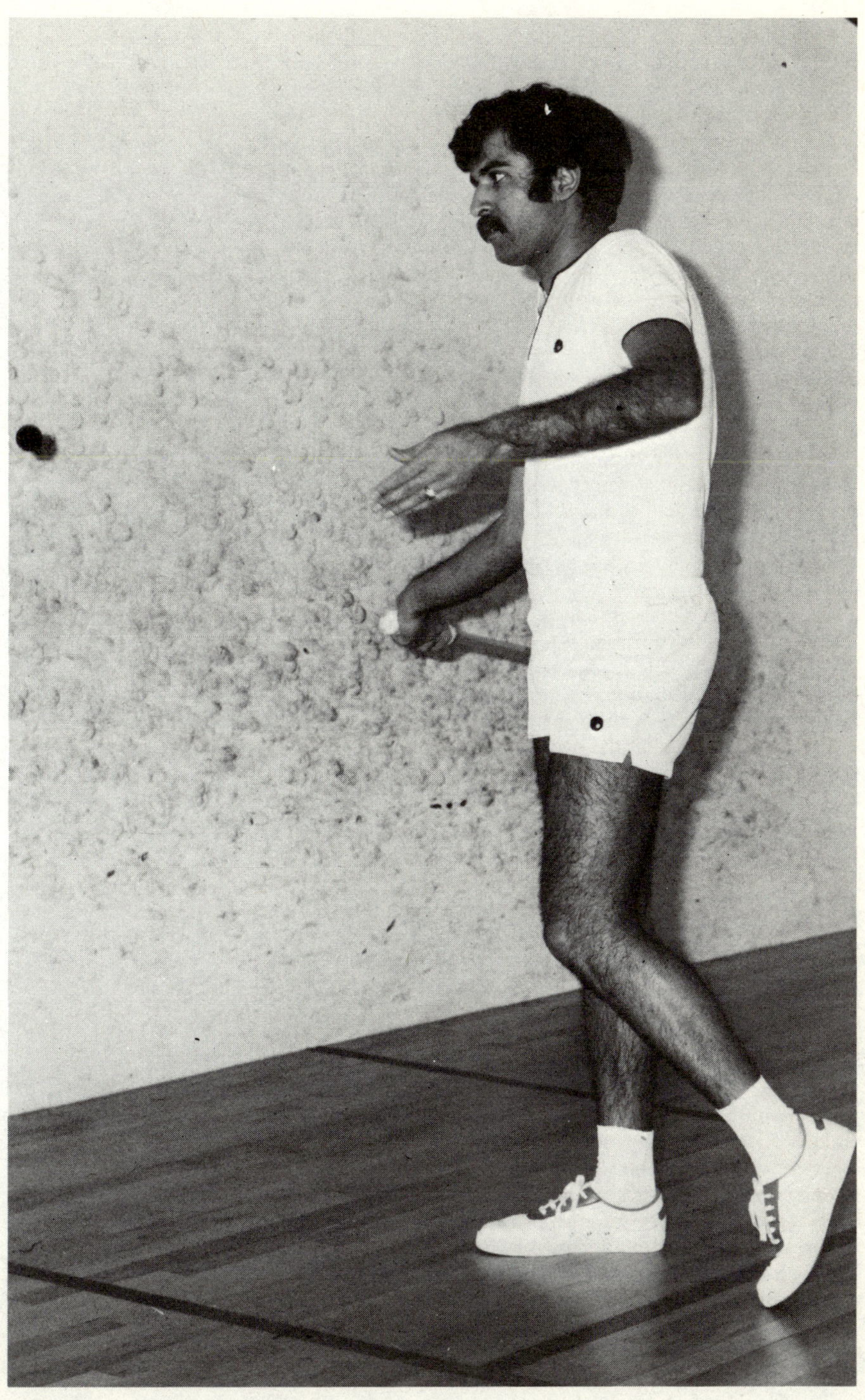

the common serve (which is struck overarm and pushed rather than smashed) both have the same destination. Despite the difference in the float of the ball between these two serves, both are aimed at striking the opposite side wall just behind the service box and quite high up. In this fashion the ball will bounce awkwardly into the back corner, coming back at the receiver. He will have to move smartly to recover the ball, or if he should choose to volley, he will be severely tested. In this way the serve can act as an inducement for error, if not as an outright ace. It is necessary to find the side wall with this type of serve, so as not to give the receiver a clear chance to volley and take the initiative.

Return of serve: wherever possible attack the serve with a volley.

The strike action of the serve should be unhurried. With at least one foot in the box (clear of all lines, say the rules) position your body at an angle to the front wall so that when impact is made with the ball, outside the leading foot, the ball will strike the front wall about two thirds the way up and in the middle of the wall in the lateral sense. The result of the shot will reveal whether or not the angle is right. Once again, there is no substitute for practice in perfecting the shot.

One problem which afflicts beginners particularly is the throw of the ball from which the stroke is produced. The throw, too, needs practice in order to put the ball on to the strings in the right place and at the right time. So, the height and position of the throw need close surveillance.

The service aimed at the opponent's body should not be overlooked, but used sparingly as a surprise packet to gain a quick point. It is particularly valuable against either a tired opponent, or one who has been lulled into expecting the flight of the common serve.

RETURN OF SERVE

Matches can be won or lost on this vital shot. It is therefore not only essential to cultivate a good service yourself, but also to have a stock reply to your opponent's best. Some top players usually play safe with the return of serve, wishing to engage the opponent in a rally, force a winning position, and plug it with an attacking stroke. The return of serve is the opening salvo in the manoeuvring for position and is invariably placed high on the front wall and pushed down the side wall.

This is wise and methodical, but squash ought to have more spontaneity in my belief, and so I treat all serves as they come. If they are loose then I will punish them, but if it is prudent I will engage in a rally. To do so I stand a little behind the service box in a position of readiness. This means my eyes do not leave the ball whilst it is in my opponent's possession. My body is turned towards the side wall ready for my stroke, and the racket is held aloft ready for any serve dished up to me.

Wherever possible, go out and attack the serve with a volley. By waiting for the ball to bounce you get caught up in the back corners and create trouble for yourself.

This is your first chance as receiver to wrest the initiative of the rally from the server, so make the most of it: be positive.

THE ANGLE

The angle shot involves the use of the side wall of the court. (The shot which retrieves the ball from the back corners with the aid of the side walls is the boast, but this is dealt with elsewhere.) The successful execution of the angle depends on your state of mind – in as much as the walls should be considered your friends. They are there to help you, contrary to the general impression of the novice that they are a hindrance.

The squash court is similar to a billiards table in the many angles which can be played. It is of benefit if you can take time to explore the court by yourself and work out the angles necessary to reach the front wall from various depths in the court, and various distances away from the side wall on to which you are striking.

The angle: the body tends to turn into the side wall rather than be parallel to it.

The uses of angled shots are many, but the two major ones are as an attacking winner, and as a shot to put your opponent out of position. To strike for the winner, first pin your opponent at the back of the court and then hit the angle so that the ball will finally lodge in the furthest corner of the court.

To move your opponent out of position using the angle, the ball can be struck from behind him or her, usually off a drive which is a little short of perfect length. By playing the angle and leaving the ball in the front of the court, you send your opponent out of the centre of the court and give yourself the opportunity to gain command.

Technically the stroke has the same basic features as a swing, although the body tends to turn into the side wall rather than be parallel to it. Depending on how close to the side wall the ball is travelling when struck, the follow-through may have to be curtailed so as not to smash the racket. Should this be the case, use a firm wrist up to the point of impact, turning the racket upwards. Keep a comfortable distance away from the ball and the side wall for the sake of your stroke and the safety of the racket.

The boast: emphasise the weight placement over the leading foot.

THE BOAST

The boast is probably the most important and frustrating shot to play when beginning squash, although it presents few problems for the experienced player.

The boast is used when you are forced into the rear corners of the court by tight length, and need to use the side wall to retrieve the ball and make a good return. To play the shot successfully you must recognise a contradiction in the technique. The further the ball goes into the corner, the further you must extract your body out of it. This applies to both the forehand and backhand shots.

If you try to place your body between the ball and the back wall you leave no room for a backswing; that back wall is in your way. As the ball bounces into the back corner, turn your body so that you face the corner, or even the back wall. Forget about the front wall, the final objective. Now you are facing away from the front wall make sure you are far enough away from both back and side walls to swing the racket freely.

Having achieved this position the shot becomes relatively simple. Play a normal swing, but emphasise the weight placement over the leading foot and bend your knees to get under the ball. Open the racket face especially if the ball is deep in the corner, in an attempt to float it out.

When striking the ball on to the side wall make sure that the racket head is behind the ball to obtain the right degree of angle. Your body position will ensure this. A greater reliance on wrist work follows as you become more confident and proficient. Also, remember to follow through on the stroke to make sure the ball carries to the front wall.

The pictures of Hiddy Jahan in this coaching section were taken by Mike Trevillion.

Hiddy Jahan (left) established a growing maturity as a match-player in 1974–75. Here he receives the congratulations of Mohibullah Khan after winning their quarter-final match in the British Open.

WHO RUNS WORLD SQUASH?

Robert Jolly

The world of squash has an elaborate hierarchy of administrative bodies by which the sport is governed. To the eye of a cynic the avenues of power and decision-making tend to mirror other political spheres, in as much as it is a case of 'who you know', and the influence of relatively small groups that dominate. This is to admit that squash administration in not wholly democratic, existing as a mixture of active decision-making groups and *en masse* apathy.

The supreme body in world squash is the International Squash Rackets Federation (ISRF) which was founded in London in January 1967, to care for the welfare of the game and settle international troubles between members. The responsibility for the rules of the game is also lodged with the ISRF together with the control of the International Amateur Championships, usually referred to as the World Amateur Championships. The founder members of the ISRF are South Africa, Australia, Great Britain, Canada, USA, Egypt, Pakistan, and India. Kuwait, Mexico, and Sweden are full members, whilst the Bahamas, Finland, Jamaica, Japan, and the Netherlands are associate members.

The European Squash Rackets Association was formed in 1973 and is of a completely different nature, though it works in collaboration with the ISRF. Whereas International Federation membership is restricted to countries having duly constituted national squash associations, the primary duty of the ESRF at this early stage in development is to promote squash across the European continent. Its membership restrictions are not nearly as stringent as the ISRF's. Although the countries and the leaders are in the main relatively inexperienced, they have tackled their problems energetically contributing much to the sense of order which will appear throughout Europe in time. The major distinctions between the ISRF and the ESRF are the spontaneity of the European body which is missing in the deliberations of the ISRF, and the stress on achieving the ends rather than exact adherence to the means. This is the reason behind the rather loose membership qualifications.

The need to develop squash regionally, a growing impatience with the ISRF, and an urge to assert independence has led to talk, following the formation of the ESRF, of a

Pan American Association which would primarily bring together the nations of the USA, Canada, and Mexico. These countries have an obvious link in their style of squash, based on different court dimensions from those recognised in the rest of the world. Such an isolationist feeling would not enhance the universal growth patterns in the sport, but are understandable in a world where geography tends to accentuate the 'us versus them' impression.

There is rumour also that an Asian Association may spring into being. Once again the lack of identity with the ISRF, and regional chauvinism could be the stimulus in the incorporation of such an Asian body.

Among the developed squash-playing nations the administrative structures are broadly run on the same lines. The lines of communication run from the individual squash player (who either belongs to an affiliated club, competes in an affiliated league competition, or holds direct membership of the squash rackets association of the country) to the club, which is grouped with others in an area association; in turn this is part of a federal system of government at the national level.

The administrations are riddled with committees, but in only very few cases are officials paid for their duties.

The rapid expansion of squash throughout the world has been highlighted in Britain, perhaps more than elsewhere, by the establishment of new and vigorous bodies linked with the commercial sphere in squash. The re-emergence of a court-owners' association, which was transformed into the British Squash Rackets Proprietors Federation (BSRPF) in 1973, was a symptom of a maturing industry which was beginning to acknowledge unashamedly that the point of being a court owner was not simply to be a jolly good fellow and provide court facilities, nor was it for pure love of the game – rather that there was an investment value in squash courts, and that an association of like-minded businessmen would be able to share their interests and troubles to mutual advantage.

It was not long before blood was let between the governing body of the sport within Britain, and the numerically small but powerful BSRPF, over the issue of affiliation fees due to the SRA. Late in 1974 the Sports Council was asked to step in to help patch up the rift which threatened to pull the competitive side of squash into pieces. The issue remained unresolved, but the bitterness and dogmatism seem to have abated, and most important, the majority of competitive squash matches have continued.

The Squash Rackets Professionals Association, which was completely revamped early in 1974, is now building a solid foundation for the professional in Britain. It organises a full calendar of competition, conferences. and examinations. The demand for teaching professionals is running at an all-time high, and the growth in supply over the next few years will depend on the efficiency of the Professionals' Association in gathering existing professionals under its wing, and introducing new blood to the finer points not only of playing the game, but in the skills of tutelage.

A small but influential number of professionals congregated in Birmingham in 1974 and introduced a new dimension to the world of squash administration, by forming the International Squash Professionals Association (ISPA). The world's leading professionals, the men who earn their living from endorsement contracts and competitive squash rather than club coaching, had begun to organise their defences against aspects of the sport that militated against their interests. This formal organisation, about a year overdue, was finally precipitated by a series of errors in administration over which the professionals had no control, but which affected their income potential.

It was not until the 1975 Open circuit in Britain that the ISPA members flexed their muscles in affirmation of their principles. In doing so, the leading players lost public sympathy and cash – lost prize-money – and set a distance between themselves and the rest of the squash administration. The dividends are not immediately apparent, but the imposition of a positive force in tournament play was necessary.

THE RULES OF THE GAME

(As approved by the International Squash Rackets Federation)

1 **The game, how played** The game of squash rackets is played between two players with standard rackets, with balls bearing the standard mark of the SRA, and in a rectangular court of standard dimensions enclosed on all four sides.

2 **The score** A match shall consist of the best of three or five games at the option of the promoters of the competion. Each game is 9 up: that is to say the player who first wins 9 points wins the game except that, on the score being called 8-all for the first time, hand-out may, if he chooses, before the next service is delivered, set the game to 2, in which case the player who first scores two more points wins the game. Hand-out must in either case clearly indicate his choice to the marker, if any, and to his opponent.

Note to Referees

If hand-out does not make clear his choice before the next service, the referee shall stop play and require him to do so.

3 **Points, how scored** Points can only be scored by hand-in. When a player fails to serve or to make a good return in accordance with the rules, his opponent wins the stroke. When hand-in wins a stroke, he scores a point; when hand-out wins a stroke, he becomes hand-in.

4 **The right to serve** The right to serve first is decided by the spin of a racket. Thereafter the server continues to serve until he loses a stroke, when his opponent becomes the server, and so on throughout the match.

5 **Service** The ball before being struck shall be thrown in the air and shall not touch the walls or floor. The ball shall be served on to the front wall so that on its return, unless volleyed, it would fall to the floor in the quarter court nearest the back wall and opposite to the server's box from which the service has been delivered.

At the beginning of each game and of each hand, the server may serve from either box, but after scoring a point he shall then serve from the other and so on alternately as long as he remains hand-in or until the end of the game. If the server serves from the wrong box there shall be no penalty and the service shall count as if served from the right box, except that hand-out may, if he does not attempt to take the service, demand that it be served from the other box.

6 **Good service** A service is good which is not a fault or which does not result in the server serving his hand out in accordance with rule 9. If the server serves one fault he shall serve again.

7 **Fault** A service is a fault (unless the server serves his hand out under rule 9):

(a) If the server fails to stand with one foot at least within and not touching the line surrounding the service box (called a foot fault)

(b) If the ball is served on to or below the cut line

(c) If the ball served first touches the floor on or in front of the short line

(d) If the ball served first touches the floor in the wrong half court or on the half-court line. (The wrong half court is the left for a service from the left-hand box and the right for a service from the right-hand box.)

8 **Fault, if taken** Hand-out may take a fault. If he attempts to do so, the service thereupon becomes good and the ball continues in play. If he does not attempt to do so, the ball shall cease to be in play provided that, if the ball, before it has bounced twice upon the floor, touches the server or anything he wears or carries, the server shall lose the stroke.

9 **Serving hand out** The server serves his hand out and loses the stroke:

(a) If the ball is served on to or below the board or out of court or against any part of the court before the front wall

(b) If he fails to strike the ball or strikes the ball more than once

(c) If he serves two consecutive faults

(d) If the ball before it has bounced twice upon the floor, or has been struck by his opponent touches the server or anything he wears or carries.

10 **Let** A let is an undecided stroke and the service or rally in respect of which a let is allowed shall not count and the server shall serve again from the same box. A let shall not annul a previous fault.

11 **The play** After a good service has been delivered the players return the ball alternately until one or the other fails to make a good return or the ball otherwise ceases to be in play in accordance with the rules.

12 **Good return** A return is good if the ball, before it has bounced twice upon the floor, is returned by the striker on to the front wall above the board without touching the floor or any part of the striker's body or clothing, provided the ball is not hit twice or out of court.

Note to Referees

It shall not be considered a good return if the ball touches the board either before or after it hits the front wall.

13 **Strokes, how won** A player wins a stroke:

(a) Under rule 9

(b) If his opponent fails to make a good return of the ball in play

(c) If the ball in play touches the striker or his opponent or anything he wears or carries, except as is otherwise provided by rules 14 and 15.

14 **Hitting an opponent with the ball** If an otherwise good return of the ball has been made, but before reaching the front wall it hits the striker's opponent or his racket or anything he wears or carries, then:

(a) If the ball would have made a good return and would have struck the front wall without first touching any other wall, the striker shall win the stroke, except that, if the striker shall have followed the ball round and so turned before making a stroke, a let shall be allowed

(b) If the ball would otherwise have made a good return, a let shall be allowed

(c) If the ball would not have made a good return, the striker shall lose the stroke.

The ball shall cease to be in play, even if it subsequently goes up.

15 **Further attempts to hit the ball** If the striker strikes at and misses the ball, he may make further attempts to return it. If after being missed, the ball accidentally touches his opponent or his racket or anything he wears or carries, then:

(a) If the striker could otherwise have made a good return, a let shall be allowed

(b) If the striker could not have made a good return he loses the stroke.

If any such further attempt is successful but the ball before reaching the front wall hits the striker's opponent or his racket or anything he wears or carries, a let shall be allowed and rule 14 (a) shall not apply.

16 **Appeals** An appeal may be made against any decision of the marker.

(a) The following rules shall apply to appeals on the service

(i) No appeal shall be made in respect of foot faults

(ii) No appeal shall be made in respect of the marker's call of 'fault' to the first service

(iii) If the marker calls 'fault' to the second service, the server may appeal and, if the decision is reversed, a let shall be allowed

(iv) If the marker does not call 'fault' or 'out of court' to the second service, hand out may appeal even if he attempts to take the ball, and if the decision is reversed, hand out becomes hand in

(v) If the marker does not call 'fault' or 'out of court' to the first service hand out may appeal if he makes no attempt to take the ball. If the appeal is disallowed, hand out shall lose the stroke

(b) An appeal under rule 12 or 16 (a) (iv) shall be made at the end of the rally in which the stroke in dispute has been played

(c) In all cases where an appeal for a let is desired, this

appeal shall be made by addressing the referee with the words, 'Let, please'

Play shall thereupon cease until the referee has given his decision.

(d) No appeal may be made after the delivery of a service for anything that occurred before that service was delivered.

17 **Fair view and freedom of stroke**

(a) After making a stroke a player must get out of his opponent's way as much as possible.

If, in the opinion of the referee, a player has not made every effort to do this the referee shall stop play and award a stroke to his opponent.

(b) When a player:

(i) Fails to give his opponent a fair view of the ball

(Note: a player shall be considered to have had a fair view unless the ball returns too close to his opponent for the player to sight it adequately for the purpose of making a stroke.)

(ii) Fails to avoid interfering with, or crowding his opponent in getting to or striking at the ball

(iii) Fails to allow his opponent, as far as his opponent's position allows him, freedom to play the ball to any part of the front wall and to either side wall near the front wall, the referee may on appeal or without waiting for an appeal allow a let; but if in the opinion of the referee a player has not made every effort to comply with these requirements of the rule, the referee shall stop play and award a stroke to his opponent.

Notwithstanding anything contained above, if a player suffers interference from or distraction by his opponent, and in the opinion of the referee, is thus prevented from making a winning return, he shall be awarded the stroke.

Note to Referees

(a) The practice of impeding an opponent's strokes by crowding or by obscuring his view is highly detrimental to the game and referees should have no hesitation in enforcing the penultimate paragraph of this rule.

(b) The words 'interfering with . . . his opponent in getting to . . . the ball' must be interpreted so as to include the case of a player having to wait for an excessive swing of his opponent's racket.

18 **Let, when allowed** Notwithstanding anything contained in these rules.

(a) A let may be allowed

(i) If, owing to the position of the striker, his opponent is unable to avoid being touched by the ball before the return is made

Note to Referees

This rule shall be construed to include the cases of the striker whose position in front of his opponent makes it impossible for the latter to see the ball or who shapes as if to play the ball and changes his mind at the last moment preferring to take the ball off the back wall, the ball in either case hitting the opponent who is between the striker and the back wall. This is not, however, to be taken as conflicting in any way with the referee's duties under rule 17.

(ii) If the ball in play touches any article lying in the court

(iii) If the player refrains from hitting the ball owing to a reasonable fear of injuring his opponent

(iv) If the player in the act of striking touches his opponent

(v) If the referee is asked to decide an appeal and is unable to do so

(vi) If the player drops his racket, calls out or in any other way distracts the attention of his opponent and the referee considers such occurrence to have caused his opponent to lose the stroke.

(b) A let shall be allowed

(i) If hand-out is not ready and does not attempt to take the service

(ii) If a ball breaks during play

(iii) If an otherwise good return has been made, but the ball goes out of court on its first bounce

(iv) As provided for by rules 14, 15, 16 (a) (iii) and 22.

(c) Provided always that no let shall be allowed

(i) In respect of any stroke which a player attempts to make, unless in making the stroke he touches his opponent; except as provided for under rules 18 (b) (ii) and (iii) and 15

(ii) Unless the striker could have made a good return.

(d) Unless an appeal is made by one of the players, no let shall be allowed except where these rules definitely provide for a let, namely rules 14(a), 14 (b) and 17 and paragraphs (b) (ii) and (iii) of rule 18.

19 **New ball** At any time when the ball is not in actual play a new ball may be substituted by mutual consent of the players or on appeal by either player at the discretion of the referee.

20 **Knock-up** The referee shall allow to either player or to the two players together for a period of five minutes during the hour preceding the start of a match for knocking up in a court in which a match is to be played. The choice of knocking up first shall be decided by the spin of a racket.

21 **Play in a match is to be continuous** After the first service is delivered, play shall be continuous so far as is practical, provided that at any time play may be suspended owing to bad light or other circumstances beyond the control of the players for such period as the referee shall decide. The referee shall award the match to the opponent of any player who, in his opinion, persists, after due warning, in delaying the play in order to recover his strength or wind, or for any other reason. However, an interval of one minute shall be permitted between games and of two minutes between the fourth and fifth games of a five-games match. A player may leave the court during such intervals, but

shall be ready to resume play at the end of the stated time. Should he fail to do so when required by the referee the match shall be awarded to his opponent. In the event of play being suspended for the day, the match shall start afresh, unless both players agree to the contrary.

Note to Referees

A player may not open the door or leave the court other than between games without the referee's permission.

22 **Duties of the marker** The game is controlled by the marker, who shall call the play and the score. The server's score is called first. He shall call 'fault' (rule 7 (b), (c), and (d)), 'foot fault' (rule 7 (a)), 'out of court', or 'not up' as the case may be. If in the course of play the marker calls 'not up' or 'out of court' the rally shall cease. If the marker's decision is reversed on appeal a 'let' shall be allowed except that if the marker fails to call a ball 'not up' or 'out of court', and on appeal, it is ruled that such was in fact the case, the stroke shall be awarded accordingly.

Any return shall be considered good unless otherwise called.

If, after the server has served one fault a 'let' is allowed, the marker shall call 'one fault' before the server serves again.

When no referee is appointed, the marker shall exercise all the powers of the referee.

23 **The referee** A referee may be appointed, to whom all appeals shall be directed, including appeals from the marker's decisions and calls. He shall not normally interfere with the marker's calling of the game except:

(a) Upon appeal by one of the players

(b) As provided for in rule 17

(c) When it is apparent to him that the marker has made a mistake in calling the game.

First Note to Referees

Notwithstanding the above, in the absence of an appeal, if it is evident that the score has been called incorrectly, the referee shall draw the marker's attention to this fact.

Second Note to Referees

When a decision has been made by the referee, he shall announce it to the players, and the marker shall repeat it with the consequent score, e.g. 'let ball', 'no let', or 'point to—'.

24 **Power of referee in exceptional cases** The referee has power to order:

(a) A player who has left the court to play on

(b) A player to leave the court for any reason whatsoever and to award the match to his opponent

(c) A match to be awarded to a player whose opponent fails to be present in the court within 10 minutes of the advertised time of play

(d) Play to be stopped in order that a player or players may be warned that their conduct on the court is leading to an infringement of the rules.

Note to Referees

A referee should avail himself of this rule as early as possible where one or other of the players is showing a tendency to break the provisions of rule 17.

25 **Colour of players' clothing** Players are required to wear white clothing. The referee's decision thereon to be final.

DEFINITIONS

Board (Tin): The expression denoting a line, the top edge of which is 19 inches (.483m) from the floor, set out upon the upper edge of a band of resonant material fixed upon the front wall and extending the full width of the court.

Cut line: A line set out upon the front wall, six feet (1.829m) above the floor and extending the full width of the court.

Game ball: The state of the game when the server requires one point to win is said to be 'game ball'.

Half-court line: A line set out upon the floor parallel to the side walls, dividing the back half of the court into two equal parts called right half court and left half court respectively.

Hand-in: The player who serves.

Hand-out: The player who receives the service.

Hand: The period from the time when a player becomes hand-in until he becomes hand-out.

Not up: The expression used to denote that a ball has not been returned above the board in accordance with the rules.

Out of court: The ball is out of court when it touches the front, sides or back of the court above the area prepared for play or passes over any cross bars or other part of the roof of the court. The lines delimiting such area, the lighting equipment and the roof are out of court.

Service box or **Box:** A delimited area in each half court from within which hand-in serves.

Short line: A line set out upon the floor parallel to and 18 feet (5.486m) from the front wall and extending the full width of the court.

Striker: The player whose turn it is to play after the ball has hit the front wall.

Time or **Stop:** Expression used by the referee to stop play.

PLAYER BIOGRAPHIES

Abbreviations:
Champ – Champion
Champs – Championships
U – University
Univs – Universities
Jnr – Junior
Invit Tourn – Invitation Tournament
Nat – National
Internat – International
Pro – Professional
N – North/Northern
S – South/Southern
W – West/Western
E – East/Eastern
R/u – Runner-up
Rep – Represented
sf – semi-final
qf – quarter-final

Alauddin, Gogi (Pakistan) No. 2 (ranked No. 3 in world)
Born in Pakistan in 1950. Lives in Lahore. 1967 Won Pakistan Jnr Champs, rep Pakistan in World Amateur Champs in Australia. 1970 Won University of Kent Champs. 1970, 1971 Won British Amateur Champs. 1971 Won S of England, won Essex Open, won Midlands Champs, won Northwood Invit, won Middx Open, won Surrey Open, won Danish Open. 1971, 1972, 1973 Won NW Open. 1973, 1975 r/u British Open. 1974 3rd British Open. 1975 Won Irish Open, 3rd in British Caledonian-Yellow Dot Grand Prix, r/u Warrington Open.

Allen, Dianne (Rhodesia) No. 2
Born Umtati 28/4/48. Lives in Salisbury. Other interests: tennis.

Armstrong, Dorothy (Ireland) Ranked No. 1 in Ulster
Born Portstewart, Co Antrim 17/10/46. Lives in Belfast. Profession: teacher of social studies. Other interests: tennis, reading, wine-making. Capped 11 times for Ireland. 1973–74 Won Irish Open, won Crawfordsburn Round Robin, sf Irish Closed. 1974–75 Won Ulster Handicap, won Crawfordsburn Round Robin, won Antrim Forum Champs, won Guinness Champs, won British Airways Champs, sf Irish Open.

Ayton, Philip Norman (Great Britain) No. 1 amateur
Born London, 26/1/47. Married with 1 daughter. Profession: stockbrokers' investment analyst. Other interests: tennis, sport. 1965–68 Won Cambridge U Champs (captain 1967–68). 1966–67 Won N of England Champs. 1967–68 Won N of England Champs, won Scottish Champs. 1968–69 Won N of England, S of England, Scottish, and Welsh Champs. 1969–70 Won S of England, won Dutch Champs, won S African Champs. 1970–71 Won Dutch Champs, won Abbeydale Invit Tourn. 1971–72 Won Dutch Champs, won Midlands Champs. 1972–73 Won Abbeydale Invit Tourn. 1973–74 Won Dutch Champs, won S African Champs. 1974–75 Won Abbeydale Invit, won S of England, won E of

GOGI ALAUDDIN

England, won Midlands. Internat matches: for England – 1st year 1968–69, total 21 caps in home internationals, 14 caps in European Champs matches over 3 years. For Great Britain – tour SA 1970 won 3 caps, 1971 World Champs NZ 5 caps; 1972–73 tour of SA 3 caps; 1973 World Champs SA 4 caps; 1974–75 tour Pakistan 3 caps. Played for Sussex since 1968.

Barbour, Neven (New Zealand) No. 1
Born Gisborne 16/1/48. Lives in Auckland. Married with 2 children. Other interests: cricket, tennis, farming. Profession: real estate. New Zealand Jnr Rep 1966. NZ Colts team 1971; NZ Men's team 1972, 1973, 1974. NZ r/u 1972; NZ Champ 1973, 1974.

Barniville, Geraldine (Ireland) No. 1 (equal 1973–74)
Born 7/11/42. Lives in Shandkill, Co Dublin. Married with 3 sons. Other interests: internat tennis player, music. Won Leinster Open 1971, 1972, 1973, 1974. Won Irish Open 1974.

Barrington, Jonah (Great Britain and Ireland) No. 1
Ranked No. 7 in the world. Born Morwenstowe, Cornwall 29/4/41. Lives in Solihull. Married with 1 son. Other interests: reading, music. Chairman ISPA. 1959 and 1964 Cornwall Champ. 1965 Won N of England, won S of England, won W of England, won Welsh Open. 1965–68 rep Ireland. 1966, 1967, 1969, 1970–72 won Open Champs. 1966–68 Won Amateur Champs. 1966, 1967, 1969 won Irish Open. 1966 Won Dutch Open. 1967–69 and 1975 rep GB. 1967 Won Egyptian Open. 1968 Won Australian Amateur, won S African Champs. 1969 Won Pakistan Nat Champs. 1970 Won North West Open, won SE of England Open, won Stockton Open, won Durham Open. 1975 8th in Yellow Dot series, won W Warwicks Champs.

Barrow, Douglas George (South Africa) No. 5
Born Johannesburg 29/9/43. Lives in Randburg. Married with 2 children. Other interests: tennis and all sports. 1963 Won Welsh Champs, SA University Champs. 1968 Won W Province Champs. 1971 Won S African, Transvaal, Border Champs. 1972 Won S African champs.

JONAH BARRINGTON

Botha, Dawie (South Africa) No. 2
Born Graaf Reinet 24/10/40. Lives in Pretoria. Other interests: history, politics. 1962 Midlands Champ. 1965 Transvaal Open Champ. 1965 Champ of Champions. 1966 Border Champ. 1966 Natal Invit Champ. 1967 SA Champ. 1967 Border Champ. 1968 N Transvaal Open Champ, Natal Invit Champ. 1969 N Transvaal Open

Champ. 1970 Border Champ, Natal Invit Champ. 1973 Champ of Champions. 1974 E Province Champ.

Bridgens, Valerie (South Africa) No. 5
Born Port Elizabeth 22/10/52. Lives in Port Elizabeth. Profession: secretary. Other interests: swimming, sport. 1970 Westview Club Champ. 1971 E Province Open Champ and Westview Club Champ. 1972 SA U23 Champ. 1973 E Province U23 Champ. 1974 E Province Open Champ, Westview Club Champ.

Broun, Howard (New Zealand) No. 3
Born Auckland 26/1/48. Lives in Auckland. Other interests: tennis (former member Davis Cup team). 1973 r/u Henderson tourn, qf NZ Men's Champs. 1974 Won Remuera Club Open, won Waika Open, won Auckland Champs, r/u Tauranga tourn, sf NZ Champs at Hamilton, r/u North Shore Invit Tourn; represented NZ v GB in Test series.

Brownlee, Bruce (New Zealand) No. 7
Born Hamilton 5/1/55. Lives in Rotorua. 1973 Capt NZ Junior team v Australia. 1974 Won North Shore Open, rep Bay of Plenty in GB. 1975 Won Solihull Open, won Rotorua Open, r/u Royal Oak Invit, r/u Eden-Epsom Invit.

Bruce-Lockhart, A. K. (Scotland) No. 1 (Rated No. 11 in GB).
Born Woking, 16/6/46. Lives in Harrow. Other interests: reading, cinema, music, philosophy, trout fishing, cricket. 1970 Won Middx Open. 1970 r/u Stockton Open. 1972 r/u Scottish Open. 1974 Won Scottish Closed, 1st reserve GB v Pakistan 1974–75. Represented Scotland since 1969.

Bucht, Harri (Finland) No. 3
Born Helsinki, 25/5/54. Lives in Helsinki. Other interests: all sports. 1974 Finnish Champ, qualified in British Amateur. Rep Finland in European Team Champs 1974–75.

Buckingham, Pamela (New Zealand) No. 2
Born Whitiora, Cambridge 8/5/46. Lives in Auckland. Other interests: tennis. 1969 Won NZ Champs, rep NZ, in Australia, won North Island Champs, ranked No. 1. 1970 Won Henderson Open, won Panmure Open, won North Island Champs, withdrew from NZ team from Australia because of health. Ranked No. 3. 1971 Won Waikato Champs, won North Shore Guinness Tourn, won N Island Tourn, won NZ Champs. Ranked No. 1. 1972 Won Waikato Champs, member of NZ team that beat GB in Auckland, and toured Australia. Ranked No. 3. 1973

Member of NZ women's team against GB, winning all internationals, sf British Women's Champs, won Remuera Open, won Waikato Open, won NZ Champs. Ranked No. 1. 1974 Played in all 3 home internationals against Australia, r/u NZ Champs, member of NZ team for visit to Australia, r/u in Waikato and Auckland Champs. Member of Auckland team.

Carlisle, Ian Trevor (Wales) No. 4
Born Swansea 29/4/54. Other interests: tennis, classical music, Russian and American literature, backgammon, Marxist economics. 1972–73 Won Welsh Jnr Champs. 1973 Won Middx Jnr Champs, won Midland U20. 1974 Won Cheshire Homes Open, won Welsh Closed. Won British Univs.

Chalmers, Robin R. (Scotland)
Born Edinburgh 6/10/47. Lives in London. Profession: accountant. Other interests: travel, light reading. 1971–72 Losing f Irish Open, won E of Scotland Champs. 1973–74 Losing f Warrington Invit and Scottish Closed, sf Wessex Champs. 1974 Won Classic Plate, won N and S Island Champs (NZ). 1974–75 losing f Wessex Champs and Warrington Invit, sf Scottish Closed. Played 27 times for Scotland.

Cogan, Peter (France) Ranked No. 3 all players
Born in England 27/4/44. Lives in St Cloud, France. Married with 3 children. Other interests: tennis, antiques. Profession: Dunlop representative. 1960–62 Kent Jnr Team. 1967 Champ of Trinidad and Tobago.

Cogswell, Sue (Great Britain) No. 1
Born Birmingham 7/9/51. Profession: physiotherapist. Other interests: reading, hockey, golf, watching football, cooking. 1973 Won Challengers Cup. 1974 r/u South of England, r/u SE England, r/u Essex Open, won Middx Open, r/u Prodorite Invit, r/u British Open, won Wessex Open, won Mercia Champs, won Belgian and Midland Open.

Colburn, Alan (South Africa) No. 8
Born in South Africa 19/1/49. Lives in Transvaal. Other interests: economics. 1971 SA Univ Champ. 1972 SA Univ Champ. 1973 SA Univ Champ. 1974 Won E of England Champ, won Wimbledon Cup, won E Transvaal Champ, won SA Champ of Champs.

Colyer, Trevor Henry (New Zealand) No. 6
Born Timaru 18/1/50. Lives in Massey, Auckland. Married, without children. Profession: production man-

ager. Other interests: golf, table tennis. 1968 NZ Jnr Champ. 1970 NZ Colts. 1972 NZ Senior. 1974–75 NZ Senior.

KEITH COPPIN

Coppin, Keith (South Africa) No. 6
Born in Port Elizabeth 27/11/44. Lives in Rosebank, Cape. Other interests: sports, music. 1968 r/u WP Champs. 1970 Won WP Champs. 1971 Won WP Champs. 1972 r/u WP Champs, won Border Champs. 1973 Won WP Champs.

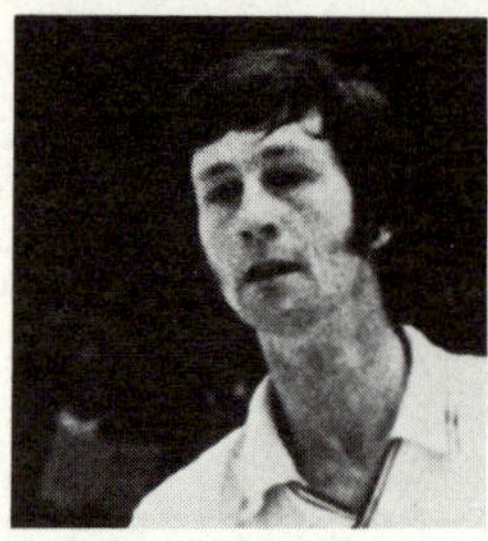

MICHAEL CORBY

Corby, Michael Wells (Great Britain) No. 2
Born Jubbulpore, India 18/2/40. Lives in London. Married. 1958 Won Drysdale Cup. 1962 Won W of England Champs. 1962, 1964, 1973, 1974 Won Middx Champs. 1963, 1968 Won Dutch Open. 1966 and 1968 Won S of England Champs. 1967, 1968 r/u British Amateur Champs. 1968 Won Welsh Open, won Mercia Open, r/u S African Champs. 1971 r/u N Zealand Open. 1973 r/u Swedish Open. 1974 r/u Abbeydale Invit. 1962–71 and 1975 rep England. 1967–71 and 1975 rep GB (total 31 caps).

Courtney, Jane (Great Britain) No. 3
Born London 2/12/48. Lives in Cardiff. Married with no children. Other interests: dressmaking, tennis. 1972–73 Won Mercia Tourn, won Surrey, r/u Midlands, r/u SE England. 1973–74 Won Belgium Open, won Wessex Open, r/u Welsh Open. 1974–75 Won Dutch Open, r/u Wessex Open.

Courtney, Stuart Hamilton (Great Britain) No. 5
Born Bushey, Herts 8/4/49. Lives in Cardiff. Married with no children. Profession: Director of industrial cleaning co. Other interests: commerce, cricket, tennis, Eton Fives, music. 7 caps for GB and 7 for England. Ranked No. 1 1973–74. UDC Rhodesia Festival 1974. 1967 Won Maidstone Open. 1968 Won Maidstone Open, won E of England, won Surrey Open, won E Sussex Open. 1969 Won Midland, won Durham & Teesside Open, won Wessex. 1970 r/u Mercia Open, r/u Wessex. 1971 Won Herts Closed. 1972 Won S of England, won Herts Closed, won Wessex Open. 1973 Won S of England, won Herts Closed, won Abbeydale Invit. 1974 r/u Midland. 1975 r/u Rolex British Closed.

Davis, Robyn (New Zealand) No. 5
Lives in Auckland. Other interests: basketball, netball, water skiing, big-game fishing. 1968 Won Tauranga Champs. 1970 Won Corbans Tourn. 1972 Won Henderson Champs, qf National Champs, Dunedin. 1973 Won N

Shore Early Times, won Henderson and Manurewa Tourns, r/u N Island Champs. 1974 Won NZ Classic Plate Hamilton, member of NZ team visiting Australia.

Easter, John (Great Britain) No. 2 professional. Ranked 16 in world.
Born in England 17/12/45. Lives in Surbiton. Turned professional April 1974. Other interests: cricket (Oxford blue), golf, music, theatre. 1968 Won Surrey Closed. 1970 Won Mercia Open. 1970–73 England and GB international 21 caps; 1973 Won NE of England. 1972 Won Belgium Open. 1972 and 1973 Won Plymouth Open. 1973 and 1974 Won Swiss Open.

Eckstein, Jill (South Africa) No. 2
Born Cape Town 8/6/46. Married with 2 daughters. Profession: tennis coach. Chairman of W Province WSRA. 1966, 1967, and 1968 Won WP Champs. 1967 Won SA Champs. 1968 Played for S Africa v GB in GB. 1970 Won WP Champs, won SA Champs. 1971 Won SA Champs, won WP Champs. 1972, 1973 Won WP Champs. 1973 Won WP Open Champs, played for SA v GB, rep SA in Australian Open Champs sf losing to Marion Jackman. 1974 Won WP Champs, won WP Open Champs, won Natal Champs.

Erskine, Gay (Rhodesia) No. 3 for SA
Born Rusape, Rhodesia 27/11/43. Lives in Salisbury. Married with 3 children. Profession: accountant. Other interests: riding, art, dressmaking, handiwork, music. 1959, 1960, 1961, 1962 Mashonaland Champ. 1963 Mashonaland Champ, Rhodesian Champ, rep SA v GB in SA. 1964 Mashonaland Champ, Rhodesian Champ. 1965 Mashonaland Champ, Rhodesian Champ, SA Champ. 1966 Mashonaland Champ, Rhodesian Champ, SA Champ. 1967 Mashonaland Champ, Rhodesian Champ, r/u SA Champ. 1968 Mashonaland Champ, Rhodesian Champ, SA Champ. Captain SA team v GB in GB. 1970, 1971, 1973 Mashonaland Champ, Rhodesian Champ. 1973 Captain SA team v GB in SA. 1974 Mashonaland Champ, Rhodesian Champ, r/u SA Champ.

Francis, T. Clive (Great Britain)
Born Wigan 6/5/42. Lives in Lytham St Annes. Married with 2 sons. Profession: tennis coach and sports retailer. Other interests: tennis, golf, cars. Ranked No. 4 before turning pro in 1967. 1963 W of England Champ. 1964, 1965, 1966 Lancs Champ. 1964, 1965 Staffs Open Champ. 1966 Midlands Open Champ. 1969 Open Plate Winner. 1967–1975 Closed British Pro Champ, 3rd

place British Pro Open 1974 and 1975. 1973, 1974 r/u W of England.

Gotto, David (Ulster) No. 2
Born Belfast 25/12/48. Profession: final year PhD student. Other interests: billiards. Ranked No. 7 in Ireland. 1972 r/u Copeland Shield Champs. 1973 Won Ulster Handicap Tourn. 1974 Plate Winner Waterford Open, Plate Winner Leinster CC Open, r/u CIYMS Invit Tourn, r/u Belfast Boat Club Tourn. 1975 r/u Ulster Open, r/u Guinness Tourn.

Grandchamp, Jean (France) (Rated No. 4 national player)
Born Paris 4/6/34. Married with 2 children. Profession: medicine. Other interests: music.

Greene, Laurie (New Zealand) No. 4
Born Hamilton 24/6/43. Other interests: tennis.
1969 Member of NZ team touring Australia. 1970 r/u Waikato Open, member of NZ team in Australia beating Ken Hiscoe in interstate series, r/u John Reid Tourn. 1971 Won Waikato Open, won Corbans Tourn, member of NZ team playing in 3rd International series, ranked No. 3. 1972 Won Manawatu Open, won Auckland Open, won NZ Champs, r/u Hughes and Cossar Tourn, ranked No. 1. 1973 Won Te Aroha Open, won Auckland Open, r/u North Island Champs, ranked No. 4. 1974 Reserve for 1st test v GB.

Grozdanovitch, Deni (France) (Rated No. 2 national player)
Born Paris 9/5/46. Profession: tennis coach. Other interests: tennis. 1975 Champ of France.

Hawkes (née Lamb) **Julie** (New Zealand) No. 4
Born Te Aroha 20/2/49. Lives in Wellington. Married to Richard Hawkes, former New Zealand Davis Cup player. Other interests: tennis and gardening. 1972 Won Wellington Open, rep NZ on Australian tour. 1973 Won North Island Champ, Wellington Open. 1974 reached sf NZ Open, won Waikato Open, won Wellington Open, rep NZ against Australia.

Hellstrom, Mikael (Sweden) No. 1
Born Stockholm 2/12/50. Lives in Lund. Student of medicine. Other interests: music, golf, literature.

Hiscoe, Ken (Australia) No. 2 (ranked No. 6 in world)
Born in 1938. Lives in Sydney. Married. 1960–64, 1966, 1967 Won Australian Amateur Champs. 1961 Won S of England, won Midlands Champs. 1962 Won British

Amateur Champs, won Scottish Amateur Champs. 1963 Won S African Champs. 1975 3rd British Open, 6th in British Caledonian-Yellow Dot Grand Prix, 3rd Warrington Open. 1967, 1969, 1971 Rep Australia in World Amateur Champs.

Hubinger, Lyle (Australia) No. 4
Born Brisbane 23/4/48. Other interests: golf, music.

Hunt, Geoffrey Brian (Australia) No. 1.
Ranked No. 2 in the world
Born 11/3/47 Melbourne. Lives in Cheltenham, Victoria. Married with 1 son. Turned pro October 1971. Other interests: fishing, swimming. 1962–65 Victoria Jnr Champ. 1963–71 Victoria Champ. 1963 Australian Jnr Champ. 1965 Scottish Amateur Champ, r/u British Amateur. 1965, 1969, 1970, 1971 Australian Amateur Champ. 1967, 1969, 1971 Internat Amateur Champ. 1969, 1974 British Open Champ. 1970, 1972 r/u British Open. 1970 British Amateur Champ. 1970, 1971 Tasmania Champ. 1971, 1972 NSW Open Champ. 1971, 1974 Australian Open Champ. 1972 SE of England Champ. 1972, 1973, 1974 Durham Open Champ. 1972, 1973 Stockton Open Champ. 1972, 1973 Grandee Open Champ. 1973, 1974 Irish Open Champ. 1974 Prodorite Open Champ, S African Champ. 1975 Warrington Open Champ, 1st Yellow Dot series.

GEOFFREY HUNT

Irving, Jennifer Elizabeth (Australia) No. 2
Born Melbourne. Lives in Kangaroo Point, Queensland. Married with 1 child. Other interests: music, tennis. Played for Victoria 1961–65. 1962 r/u Australian Champ. 1963 Manager Australian U21 team. 1968 r/u Queensland Champ. 1969 r/u Australian Champ. 1970 r/u Australian Champ. 1971 r/u British Champ. 1971, 1972 r/u Queensland Champ. 1972 r/u Australian Champ. 1972 W Australian Champ, r/u Victorian Champ and NSW Champ. 1973, 1974 r/u Queensland Champ. 1974 r/u Australian Champ, Brisbane Champ.

MARION JACKMAN

Jackman, Marion June (Australia) No. 1
Born in Brisbane. Lives in Brisbane. Married with no children. Other interests: music, surfing, home and garden, tennis. Rep Queensland 1963–1974 inc. Rep Australia 1965, 1967, 1971, 1972, 1975. Queensland Champ 1964–1974 inc. Brisbane Champ 1964, 1965, 1967–1973 inc. N Queensland Champ 1968–1974 inc. R/u Australian Champ 1966–1968 inc, 1971, 1973. 1974 Australian Champ.

Jahan, Hiddy (Pakistan) (ranked No. 4 in world)
Born in Quetta 1950. Lives in London. Married. Turned pro January 1974. 1971, 1972 Won Swedish International Champs. 1971–73 Won Welsh Open. 1971, 1972 Won N of England. 1972 Won Middx Open, won Wimbledon Open. 1973 Won Mercia Open. 1974 sf British Amateur Champs. 1975 r/u N W Open, r/u Irish Open, won Chichester Open, 4th in British Open, 2nd in British Caledonian-Yellow Dot Grand Prix.

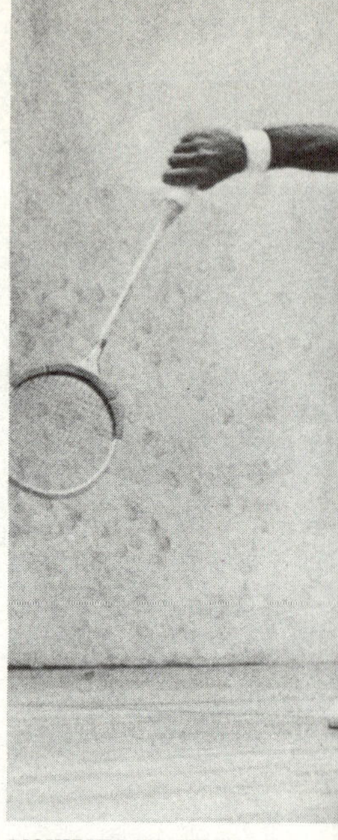
MOHIBULLAH KHAN

Johnston, Trevor (New Zealand) No. 2
Born 15/12/41. Lives in Rotorua. Married with 2 sons. Other interests: music, cars. 1966 Won NZ Champ. 1967 Member NZ team v Australia. 1968 Won NZ Champ. 1969 Member NZ team, won SA Invit Tourn. 1971 Member NZ team, won triallists' tourn at Henderson, won NZ triallists' tourn at N Shore, won Manawatu Open. 1972 Won Waikato Open, won Guinness tourn N Shore, won Panmure Open, won Hughes and Cossar tourn Eden Epsom Club, Auckland, won Corbans tourn. 1973 Won N Island Champs, won Hughes and Cossar tourn, won Corbans tourn. 1974 Won N Island Champs, won Bay of Plenty, won Manawatu Open, sf NZ Champs, member of NZ team beating GB, member of NZ team v Australia.

Jones, Roger (Finland) No. 1
Born Walsall, England 24/9/43. Lives in Kauniainen, Finland. Married with 2 children. Other interests: reading. Winner of all tournaments played in Finland since 1970. 1971 qf Middlesex Open. 1972 Won Swedish Open Plate, qf Wimbledon Champs. Rep Finland in European team champs 1974–75.

Jude, David (Wales) No. 1
Born Ipswich 17/2/39. Lives in Eastcombe, nr. Stroud. Married with 3 children. Profession: banker. Other interests: tennis. 1953, 1954 Won Junior Evans Cup. 1956 Won Drysdale Cup, won Evans Cup. 1967 Won Gloucester Champs. 1975 Rep Wales in European Champs.

Kenyon, Philip Stephen (Great Britain)
Born Blackpool 7/5/56. Lives in Rickmansworth. Profession: scientific officer. Other interests: surfing, tennis, motoring, swimming. 1972, 1973, 1974, 1975 Lancs and Cheshire Jnr Champ. 1974, 1975 British Jnr Champ (closed U19). 1974 British Jnr Open Champ, won Yellow Dot Champ of Champs, won Surrey Jnr Open Champs. Toured S Africa with SRA Seniors. Area finalist Harp Lager tourn 1974, inter-area finalist 1975. 1975 Lancs Senior County Closed Champ.

Khan, Mohibullah (Pakistan) No. 1
Born Peshawar 5/1/56. Lives in Peshawar. Other interests: tennis. 1968 U16 Jnr Champ. 1970–72 Won Nat Jnr Champs. 1971 Won Drysdale Cup, rep Pakistan in international series in NZ. 1973 f Nat Amateur and Open. 1973–74 Won British Amateur. 1974 Won Pakistan Open, f Egypt Open and Singapore Open, Viking Champ. 1974–75 British Amateur Champ. 1975 r/u Durham Open.

Khan, Rehmat (Pakistan)
Born Peshawar 30/10/44. Married with 2 children. 1964 r/u Pakistan Open.

Khan, Rehmatullah (Pakistan) No. 6
Born Karachi 8/2/51. Turned pro 1971. Son of Nazrullah Khan. Other interests: tennis. 1972 Won W of England Open Champs. 1973 r/u W of England Open Champs. 1972–74 r/u Plymouth Open Champs. 1972 r/u Australian Pro. 1974 r/u Mercia Open.

Khan, Torsam (Pakistan) No. 4
Born Rawalpindi 27/9/51. Lives in London. Turned pro 1/1/73. Other interests: tennis. 1967 Won U16 Nat Champs. 1971 Rep Pakistan in internat series in NZ. 1972 Won W of England Open. 1973 r/u Mercia Open, r/u Welsh Open, r/u E Anglia, won Wimbledon Stadium Open, won Harp Lager Open. 1974 Won NE of England, won Mercia Open Champs, won Welsh Open, r/u W of England Open. 1975 7th in Yellow Dot series.

Kirton, Pat G. (Great Britain)
Born Bexhill, Sussex 30/12/36. Lives in Barnes, London. Married with 2 children. Profession: accountant/computing. Other interests: tennis, theatre, reading, travel. Played many times for England and toured S Africa with British team in 1970. Capt Middx to 4 consecutive titles, now plays for Sussex. Was Chairman SRA Champs Committee for several years. 1962 Won Isle of Wight Champs. 1961 Won Essex Champs. 1967, 1968 Won Middx Champs. 1968, 1969 Won Wimbledon Cup. 1969 Won Surrey Open, won Swedish Internat. 1971 Won Harp Lager. 1975 Won Belgian Champs, rep England in European Champs.

Lawes, Teresa Mary (Great Britain) No. 4
Born Beckenham, Kent 27/2/48. Profession: GLC Clerical Officer. Other interests: opera, ballet, concerts, theatre. 1969, 1971 r/u NZ Champs. 1970 Won NZ Champs. 1973–74 Won Mercia Champs, won Essex Champs, won Kent Champs. 1974–75 r/u Mercia Champs, won Welsh Champs, won Scottish Champs, won W of England Champs.

STEPHANIE LYNAS

Leslie, Jonathan C. A. (Great Britain) No. 6
Born Kasulu, Tanzania 13/12/50. Lives in Beaconsfield, Bucks. Profession: barrister. Other interests: tennis (cap Oxford), rackets, fives, bridge. 1971–74 Bucks Champ. 1972 r/u British Univs. 1973 r/u British Univs. 1972–73 Played No. 1 for Oxford U. 1973–74 Played London Squash (Cumberland and Bath). 1974–75 Won Univ of Kent, r/u Swiss Open to John Easter, won Rolex British Amateur Closed.

Lynas, Stephanie (Ireland)
Born Belfast 7/11/44. Lives in Lisburn, Co Antrim. Married with 1 son. Other interests: tennis, hockey. 1972 Won Women's Irish Open. 1973 r/u Crawfordsburn Round Robin Tourn. 1974–75 Won Ulster Closed Champs, won Belfast Boat Club Invit, r/u Crawfordsburn Round Robin Tourn.

Machet, Selwyn (South Africa) No. 4
Born Johannesburg 5/7/46. Married with 1 child. Other interests: golf, tennis, table tennis. 1971 Won Natal Invit. 1972 Won Scottish Champs. 1973 Won World Plate. 1974 Won Natal Invit, won Johannesburg Club Invit, f SA. Amateur.

MacDonald, Graham Frank (South Africa) No. 9
Born Johannesburg 13/6/43. Lives in Shipley, Yorkshire, UK. Profession: lecturer in philosophy. Other interests: music, chess. Turned professional Feb 1974. 1969 Won Natal Invit. 1969 r/u Transvaal Champs. 1970 Won Transvaal Champs, r/u SA Champs. 1966–70 Played for S Africa 13 times. 1970 r/u Midlands Open Champs. 1971 Captain Oxford U team.

McIntyre, Cecilie (New Zealand) No. 3
Born Auckland 6/6/46. Lives in Rotorua. Married, no children. Other interests: tennis. 1966 Won Auckland Champs, rep NZ in Australia. 1967 Won Auckland Champs, rep NZ in Australia, ranked No. 2. 1969 qf British Women's Amateur (losing to Heather McKay). 1970 Won Guinness Tourn, Auckland, rep NZ in Australia. 1972 Won NZ Champs, won N Shore Tourn, won Auckland Champs, won N Island Champs, rep NZ v GB, rep NZ on tour of Australia, ranked No. 1. 1973 No. 1 player in NZ women's tour of Britain, r/u British Women's Tourn, r/u National Women's final, ranked No. 2. 1974 Won Auckland Champs, member NZ team v Australia in NZ, sf NZ Champs.

JOHN MAGRATH

McKay, Heather P. (Australia) No. 1
Born Queanbeyan, NSW 31/7/41. Married, no children. Turned professional 17/1/74. Other interests: hockey, reading, swimming. 1962–75 inc British Champ. 1960–1973 inc Australian Champ. 1961–73 NSW Champ. 1961–73 inc Victorian Champ.

Magrath, John (Ireland) No. 1
Born Belfast 17/1/47. Lives in Belfast. Married with 1 son. Profession: architect. Other interests: tennis (6 international caps, 2 Davis Cup), rugby (Ulster inter-provincial trials). 1973–74 Won Irish Closed, won CIYMS Invit Tourn, won Leinster Cricket Club Champs. 1974–75 Won Irish Closed, won CIYMS Invit Tourn, won Leinster CC Champs, won Antrim Forum Invit, r/u Waterford Open, won Guinness Trophy.

Marshall, C. E. (Kenya) No. 6
Born Kenya 12/5/30. Lives in Sheffield, England. Married with 1 child. Other interests: tennis, riding, golf, mountaineering. 1961 Won British Women's Open. 1957, 1966 Won Midland Open. 1958, 1970 Won Scottish Open. 1958–75 inc Won Yorkshire Closed. 1951, 1955 Kenya Champ. 1963 S African Champ.

Martin, Neil D. T. (Scotland) No. 2 (rated No. 15 in GB)
Born Zambia 10/8/52. Lives in London. Profession: medical student. Other interests: hill walking, travel. 1968–69 Scottish U18 Champ. 1971 Surrey Jnr U19 Champ. 1971–73 Scottish U21 Champ. 1971–74 Scottish Univs Champ. 1971 sf BUSF, 1972 f BUSF, 1973 f BUSF, 1974 r/u BUSF. 1972–73 E of Scotland Champ. 1973–74 W of Scotland Champ. 1973–74 N of Scotland Champ. 1975 Scottish Amateur Closed Champ.

Murray, Carol (Australia)
Born Australia 5/3/49. Lives in Sydney. Married, no children. Other interests: golf, travel. 1966 r/u Australian Junior Champ. 1966 r/u NSW Junior Champ. 1967 Won Australian Junior Champ. 1967 Won NSW Jnr Champ.

Millman, Paul (Great Britain) No. 10
Born Cheltenham 23/6/46. Lives in London. Other interests: tennis, cricket. 1963 Won S of England Jnr Champ. 1966 Won Zambia Champs. 1966, 1968–70 inc Won W of England Champs. 1967 Won S of England Champs, won Isle of Wight Champs. 1968 Won Essex Champs. 1969, 1970 Won Harp Lager Tourn. 1969, 1971 sf British Amateur. 1971 Won Mercia Open. 1968–75 38 caps for GB and England.

Nancarrow, Mavis Jane (Australia) No. 2 Pro
Born Harbord, Sydney 8/5/43. Married with 1 son. Turned pro May 1974. Other interests: golf, ballet, dancing, philately, needlework, surfing. 1965 New England Champ, Arndale. 1966 r/u Queensland Amateur Champs. 1966–73 inc Rep NSW. 1972 Won N District Champs. 1973 Won NSW Open Champs, r/u NSW Amateur Champs, won Eastern District Champs.

Nancarrow, Cameron John (Australia) No. 3
Ranked No. 8 in world
Born Sydney 9/4/46. Married with 1 son. Turned pro Sept 1973. Other interests: golf, surfing, tennis, music, commerce. 1963 NSW Jnr Champ. Member of winning Australian team world titles 1967, 1969, 1971, 1973. Rep Australia 1965, 1966, 1967, 1969, 1971, 1972, 1973. 1966 Won SA Amateur. 1967 r/u World Amateur. 1967, 1968, 1970, 1972 Won NSW Amateur. 1969 r/u British Open. 1970 Won Scottish Amateur, won NSW Open, won S Australia Open. 1971 r/u World Amateur. 1972 Won British Amateur, won Canadian Amateur, won Australian Amateur. 1973 Won World Amateur, won SA Amateur. 1974 r/u World Open, r/u Australian Pro. 1975 Finished 5th in Yellow Dot series.

SUE NEWMAN

Newman, Sue (Australia) No. 3
Born Sydney 24/4/50. Lives in Sylvania Waters, NSW. Other interests: riding, swimming. 1968 Won NSW Champs, won Australian Jnr Champs. 1970–72 inc Won NSW U23 Champs. 1974 Won NSW Champs.

Nierop, Christine van (Australia) No. 6
Lives in Cottesloe, Western Australia. Other interests: swimming, tennis, athletics, music. 1972 r/u Western Australia Champs. 1973, 1974 Won Western Australia Champs. 1974 r/u NSW Champs.

Nuttall, Ian (Great Britain) No. 8
Born Dover 12/8/47. Lives in York. Other interests: model railways, cricket, sport. 1968–69 UAU Champ. 1969 Won Durham County Champs. 1968–72 Won Lincs County Champs. 1971–73 Won Yorks Champs. 1973 Capt York team – Banbury Cup. 1973 Londonderry Cup. 1974 English Internat, SRA tour to S Africa. 1973–74 Churchillians (Aust, NZ). 1975 Capped for European Champs, but withdrew through injury.

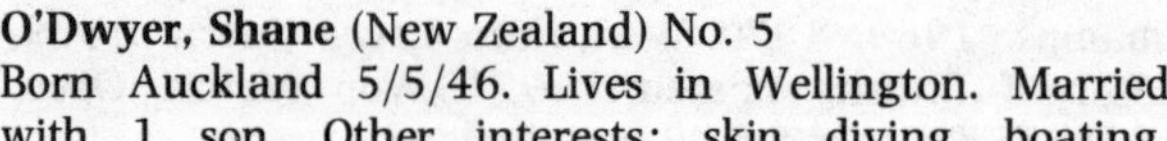

O'Dwyer, Shane (New Zealand) No. 5
Born Auckland 5/5/46. Lives in Wellington. Married with 1 son. Other interests: skin diving, boating.

THE NANCARROWS

CHRISTINE VAN NIEROP

Players' rep on NZ management committee. 1967 Visit Australia. 1969 NZ rep to Australia. 1970 Selected for NZ team in Australia. 1972 Won Wellington Champs. 1973 Won Wellington Champs, played for NZ in internat series in S Africa. 1974 Won Wellington Champs.

Patterson, Bryan (Great Britain)
Born Coventry 26/1/46. Lives in Walsall. Turned pro Jan 1974. Other interests: guitar. 1964 Won Drysdale Cup. 1964–67 Won York City Champs. 1971–74 Won Warwicks Champs. 1973 r/u World Amateur, rep England in European Team Champs. 1974 r/u NE England Champs, sf Mercia Open, won Londonderry Cup. 1975 Won Harp Lager.

Payne, Jeremy (France) No. 1
Born Cape Town 15/9/49. Lives in Paris. Other interests: tennis, golf, waterskiing, cricket. Profession: works for international mining company based in Paris.

Reedman, W. (Australia) No. 4
Born Beenleigh, Queensland 9/2/49. Lives in Sydney. Married, no children. Turned pro Sept 1973. 1967 Won Australian Jnr Champs. 1969 Won NSW U23 Champs. 1970 r/u British Amateur. 1972 r/u British Amateur. 1972 r/u Scottish Amateur.

Richardson, John Lewis (Great Britain) No. 3
Born Calcutta, India 22/1/51. Lives in Croydon, Surrey. Profession: computer programmer/operator. Other interests: photography, sport, computers, reading. 1966 Won Jnr Challenge Cup, won Bath Club, London. 1967 Won Jnr Sussex Champs, won Jnr Middx Champs, won Jnr S of England Champs. 1968 Won Jnr Sussex Champs, won Jnr Middx Champs, won Lonsdale Cup (doubles with R. Anjema). 1969 Won Jnr S of England Champs, won Drysdale Cup. 1970 Won Bristol Open, won Middx and Surrey Men's Champs. 1971 Won Bristol Open. 1972–73 Played for GB v S Africa. 1974–75 Won Warrington, won N of England and W of England. Played for GB v Pakistan.

Robinson, Ian (Great Britain) No. 7
Born in York 12/9/52. Studying PE and English (Loughborough Colleges). Other interests: sport, cricket (won East Yorks Cup), music (plays guitar and piano), photography, travel. 1969 r/u Jnr Evans. 1971 r/u Drysdale Cup. 1971 Won Yorks Jnr Cup. 1974 Won Yorks Champs, won S

Island (NZ) Champs. 1973 Churchillian tour Australia/NZ. 1974 SRA tour S Africa and NZ. 1975 rep England in European Champs.

Robberds, Gregory Mervyn (Australia) No. 7
Born Sydney 14/5/43. Lives in Carlton, NSW. Other interests: sports, tennis. Turned pro Oct 1974. 1970 qf Australian Champs. 1970–73 Won Parramatta Champs NSW, qf NSW Amateur. 1970–74 Member NSW team. 1971–74 Won Interstate Champs at Australian Champs. 1973 qf Australian Open.

Safwat, Ahmed (Egypt) No. 1 (ranked No. 9 in world)
Born Cairo 6/6/47. Lives in Sheffield. Married with 1 son. Other interests: all sports, reading, travel, chess, cars. Pro at Abbeydale. Turned pro 1971. Egyptian Jnr Champ at U16 and U19. 1962 Woń Middx Jnr Champ. 1972 Won Mercia Open. 1972, 1973 Won Harp Lager. 1973 Won NE of England. 1973, 1974 British Pro Champ. 1975 4th in Yellow Dot series, r/u West Warwickshire, won East Anglian, r/u Chichester Open.

Saleem, Mohammed (Pakistan)
Born Delhi 1945. Lives in Peshawar. Married with 3 children. Other interests: tennis, cricket. 1967 Won Pakistan Open. 1968 r/u Pakistan Open. 1971 Won Pakistan Open. Member of Pakistan team that reached f in World Champs. 1974 Won East Anglian Open, sf British Amateur. 1974–75 Capt Pakistan test team.

Salinson, Peter (France) No. 2 (all players)
Born Norwich 31/12/39. Married with 3 children. Profession: data processing. 1959, 1960, 1962 Norfolk County Champ.

Salo, Harri (Finland) No. 2
Born Helsinki 7/7/48. Married with 2 children. Profession: Secretary Finnish SRA. Other interests: music, reading, sport. 1970–72 Finnish Champ. 1973, 1974 r/u Finnish Champs. 1971 sf Kent U Champs. Qualified in British Amateur 1972 and 1974.

Salmon, Remy (France) No. 5 (nationally)
Born Paris 21/11/44. Profession: surgeon.

Sanderson, Barbara (Ireland)
Born Armagh, N Ireland. Lives in Romford, Essex. Married with 2 children. Profession: research biochemist. Other interests: modern languages, theatre, hill climbing. 1964, 1965 f Irish Open. 1968 Won

Challenge Cup, won Essex Closed. 1969 Won Irish Open. 1970 Won Essex Closed. 1971 Won Essex Open, won E of England, r/u Essex Closed. 1973, 1974 r/u Essex Closed. 1974 Won Irish Closed, r/u Irish Open.

Scott, Dave (South Africa) No. 5
Born Uitenhage, SA 10/6/50. Lives in Johannesburg. Profession: accountant. Other interests: golf, tennis. 1972 sf SA Univs. 1974 f Transvaal Champs, qf SA Champs. 1971–72 Knights Tour. 1972–73 SA Univs tour. 1975 Won Wimbledon Champs (England), r/u Scottish Champs.

Shapland, Rhonda Mary (Australia) No. 1 Junior
Born Toowoomba 6/2/58. Lives in Clontarf, Queensland. Other interests: basketball, swimming. 1971 Queensland U17 and U19 Champ, won Darling Downs B Grade Champ. 1972 Won Darling Downs Jnr Champ, won Brisbane Jnr Champ, won Australian Jnr Champ. 1973 Won Darling Downs Jnr Champ, won Queensland Jnr Champ, won N Queensland Champs, won Far N Queensland Jnr Champs, sf Australian Champs. 1974 Won Darling Downs Jnr Champ, won Brisbane Jnr Champs, won Queensland Jnr Champ, won Australian Jnr Champ, won Auckland U17 Champ.

Sherren, Stephen Wray (Rhodesia) Ranked No. 3 in SA
Born Binoura, Rhodesia 10/11/46. Other interests: tennis. 1970–73 Rhodesian Champ. 1968–75 Rep Rhodesia. 1971–73 Rep South Africa.

Stevens, John (New Zealand)
Born Auckland 27/6/43. Lives in Mt Eden, Auckland. Other interests: tennis, golf, athletics, running. 1967 Won Auckland Champs. 1968 Won Waikato Champs, won Northland Champs. 1969 Won Auckland Champs, r/u National Champs. 1971 Won Auckland Champs. 1973 Member NZ team in 4th internat amateur series v S Africa. Not ranked in 1974 because of insufficient performances. For previous 10 years ranked in first 10.

STEPHEN SHERREN

Swift, Anthony (Great Britain)
Born Liverpool 14/7/42. Lives in Bedford. Married with 2 children. Other interests: tennis, golf, photography, music, gardening. Turned pro Sept 1972. 1969–72 Won Solihull Open. 1970–71 Won Zambia Open, won E Sussex Open. 1969–72 Won Lancs Champs. 1971–72 Won W Sussex, won Scottish Open, won Maidstone Open, won NE of England.

Timperley, James Philip (South Africa) No. 10
Born Cape Town 22/1/43. Lives in Randburg, Transvaal. Married, no children. Other interests: golf. 1971, 1972, 1973 Won E Transvaal Invit. 1972, 1973, 1974 Won Natal U Invit. 1973 Won Natal Open Invit. 1973, 1974 Won Border Champs.

Vatimbella, Aris (Monaco)
Born Alexandria, Egypt 2/2/16. Lives in Monaco. Married with 2 children. Other interests: tobogganing, sailing, skiing (Olympics 1956). 1951 Won Nat Champs Greece. 1952 Won Internat Champs Greece. 1953 Won Internat Champs Greece. 1968 Won Nat Champs Monaco.

Verow, Peter Graham (Great Britain) No. 4
Born in Co Durham 20/5/53. Lives in London. 4th year medical student. Other interests: travel, sport. 1969 Won Drysdale Cup. 1970 f Drysdale Cup, losing to Mohibullah. 1971 Won Drysdale Cup. 1972 Won British Univs Champs, first played for England. 1972–74 Won Durham County Champs. 1974 Won Belgium Open, won Dutch Open, first played for GB.

PETER VEROW

Watson, Roland (South Africa) No. 1
Ranked 11th in world
Born Johannesburg 5/2/46. Lives in Pretoria. Married with 2 children. Turned pro 7/11/73. Other interests: tennis. 1965–67 Won N Transvaal Closed. 1966 Won Transvaal U21. 1967 Won N Transvaal Open. 1969–74 Won N Transvaal Closed. 1970–74 Won N Transvaal Open. 1973–74 Won Transvaal Open. 1973 UDC Festival Round Robin.

ROLAND WATSON

Webster, Jenny (New Zealand) No. 1
Born New Plymouth, Taranaki, NZ 11/3/42. Lives in Auckland. Married with 3 sons. Other interests: all sports, athletics, tennis, hockey. 1969 Member of NZ team touring Australia. 1970 r/u Nat Champs, won Manawatu Open, member of NZ team for Australian tour. 1972 r/u Nat Champs, member of NZ team v GB in NZ. 1973 Won Auckland Champs, member of NZ team for tour of GB. 1974 Won NZ Champs, won S Island Champs, r/u N Island Champs, member of NZ team for Australian tour.

QAMAR ZAMAN

Wilson, Christopher Michael Noble (Scotland) No. 3
Born Edinburgh 1/5/49. Profession: Army officer. Other interests: cross-country skiing, hill walking, travel. 1965

Won Scottish Jnr Champs. 1966 Won Scottish Jnr Champs. 1971 Won Army Champs, won Maidstone Open, won Isle of Wight Open. 1972 Won Army Champs, won 23 caps for Scotland incl 2 European Champs 1973 and 1975.

Wilson, Jean Mary (Great Britain) No. 2
Born Manchester 6/10/42. Lives in South Africa. Married. Other interests: tennis, driving, bridge. 1973–74 Won Welsh Champs, won N of England Champs, won NW Champs, won Midland Champs, won W of England. 1974–75 Won NW Champs, won N of England, won S of England.

Wilson, Peter (Wales) No. 5
Born Weston-super-Mare 9/8/44. Lives in Oxford. Profession: school teacher. Other interests: all sports. 1973–1974 Oxford County Champ.

Wright, David Henry (Australia) No. 2
Born Brisbane 17/6/41. Married with 1 child. Other interests: tennis, cricket, horse-racing. 1970–73, 1975 Won Queensland Champs. Rep Australia in N America Feb–Mar 1972; rep Australia in S Africa 1973; rep Queensland since 1969, Australia since 1971.

Yasin, Mohammed (Pakistan) No. 7 (ranked No. 15 in world)
Born Peshawar 1941. Married with 3 children. A squash professional for 20 years. 1964, 1973 Won Pakistan National Open. 1963 Won Karachi Open. 1966 Won W Pakistan Open, 4 times sf British Open. 1974 f British Open (withdrew through injury).

Zachariah, Margaret L. (Australia) No. 5
Born Melbourne. Other interests: music, gardening, diagnostic radiographics. 1971 Won Tasmanian State Champs, r/u to Heather McKay Victorian State Champs and NSW State Champs. 1973 Won Tasmanian State Champs. 1974 Won Victorian State Champs.

Zaman, Qamar (Pakistan) No. 1. Ranked No. 1 in world
Born Quetta 11/4/51. Lives in Peshawar. Other interests: tennis. 1968 Won Pakistan Jnr Champs. 1973 Won Pakistan Amateur Champs, won Australian Amateur Champs. 1973–74 Won Singapore Open, f British Amateur Champs. 1974 Won Egypt Open, sf British Open Champs, r/u British Amateur. 1975 Won Rolex NW Open, British Open, Durham Open.

ALL-TIME GREATS

Robert Jolly

Subjectivity is the ruination of comparisons. Having opened with such a maxim – home-grown to boot – how then can a list of all-time greats be compiled? The immediate response is to start with the unassailable choice of Hashim Khan, and thereafter rely on discretion.

Hashim Khan's pride of place is earned by a record seven British Open victories amongst the 45 major titles he collected in a remarkable career.

Born in 1916 near Peshawar, Pakistan (it was then India) and now resident in the USA, Hashim Khan not only dominated world squash from 1950 for the next seven years, but he established such a margin of superiority that rivals on the record books have never achieved on the court. Witness Jonah Barrington's six Open victories, yet he was beaten consistently by other players during his reign: but more of him later. He serves in this instance to illustrate why Hashim stands alone, unchallenged, as The Greatest.

The colourful story of Hashim Khan's rise to eminence begins with a career as an eight-year-old fetching the balls which strayed from the open-air squash court at the Officers' Club in the British Army's cantonment at Peshawar. Although Hashim practised and practised, he was 28 before being offered an appointment as a coach. He came to notice by winning the All-India Championships, but the partition of the sub-continent halted his opportunities to show up.

After Bari performed creditably on behalf of India in the British Open, Pakistan searched for a player of their own who could win fame for the new nation. Hashim Khan came to the fore, but only just, and was packed off to London for the mighty British Open which had been dominated by Egypt's Mahmoud Karim on four occasions, a player who had been unbeaten for a decade.

Their meeting in the final of the Open was a classic contrast in styles. Karim, noted for his elegance of movement and strokes to the point where some members of the press had been moved to call his squash perfect, was pitted against a man five years his senior (Hashim was 35), with no international experience to speak of, and a physique marked by a barrel-chest and billiard table legs.

The Pakistani conceded the first five points but in doing so extracted the sting from Karim's game and then demolished him without further loss of points, with a combination of severe drives and incredible alacrity.

Hashim's eye was so sharp that when he played a fierce skimming drive above the tin it was a 'normal' shot: for other players it was a 'chance' thing. Perhaps the greatest stroke of Hashim's game was the nick shot which he produced with uncanny regularity.

The living legend has a brother, Azam, who succeeded him at the top. Azam was a tennis professional converted to squash at his brother's instigation. Another compact player, Azam had different strengths; although he could not match Hashim for speed, he varied his game with more touch shots. He won the British Open on four occasions to complete a decade of Pakistan hegemony.

There was one interruption to the brothers' rule during the fifties. In 1956 a cousin, Roshan Khan, took the title. Roshan played an exciting game with aesthetic drop shots from ground strokes and volleys equally. Possessed of a finer and taller stature than either Hashim or Azam, Roshan had an air of elegance which, combined with his devastating shots, left a great impression in the minds of all those who saw him play.

Azam Khan bowed out after his 1961 triumph in the Open to be succeeded by another relation, Mohibullah Khan, in 1962. The young Mohibullah was a forceful player, but was seen too little in Britain to take a place in the history books – although he was to lead the American game for many years with Hashim and Hashim's son Sharif.

The periods before and after Pakistan's golden age (1950–62) were ruled by the Egyptians. Indeed, between 1935 and 1949 two Egyptians outclassed all opposition, with one exception. Amr Bey, five times Open Champion, was followed by England's James Dear for only one year before World War II sent the sport into recession. In 1946 Karim came to power, his reign continuing until his demise at the hands of Hashim four years later.

Bey was an outstanding lawn tennis player whose slight build and incredible suppleness was particularly suited to squash. He won six British Amateur championships apart from his five Open titles in a remarkably short career. He took his first amateur title after playing the game for only five years, and retired six years later at the premature age of only 28! His style of play was attacking, which was aided by his great speed to the front of the court.

Bey, who was later to become Egyptian Ambassador to the Court of St James, exerted one major influence on behalf of squash. It was he, more than anyone else, who showed by example that squash was a great game in its own right, not simply a time-filler until the rackets court was available. This accolade reflects on the skill and demeanour of the champion even more than his championship success.

Following the Khans' control of squash was the short, genial personality with mercurial strokes by the name of Abou Taleb. Young Abou was too small for tennis (his elder brother is a tennis professional) so was apprenticed at squash to Dardir. Dardir was unfortunate in having to compete against the Khans, and inevitably ran second or third despite enormous talent. When this was channelled into coaching and instruction, he brought Egypt into the limelight and helped mould the Australian style of squash which was to emerge some five years later.

The challenge of living the underdog life brought maximum effort out of Taleb – it even led him to the extent of

Below: Ken Hiscoe has never won the Open title, but his contribution to Australian squash has probably been as great as his colleague Geoff Hunt's. His superb range of strokes and aggressive style make him one of the game's most exciting competitors.

Right: Heather McKay of Australia – a legendary name from the world of squash. Her record is awesome and is never likely to be matched.

pushing his old car across the sand dunes for training. Such physical training linked with a certain devilry conjured up by deceptive wrist-work brought Taleb three world crowns. His world crashed in 1966 when Jonah Barrington, playing for Ireland, came to power by disposing of him in four stormy games.

Barrington was only the third British player to win the premier event of the game invented in England. James Dear, who took the 1938 Open title, was runner-up on no less than five occasions. Dear added five British Professional titles to his squash career, but also excelled at other sports, being Open Champion at real tennis and rackets as well as squash.

Barrington however was a specialist. After a dissipated university life followed by an aimless spell, Barrington became hooked on squash. He gave up virtually everything else to devote his energies and time to the sport. In doing so he created an aura which the newspapers lapped up. 'The monk of the West End' was a good story, and squash badly needed publicity.

Success came Barrington's way in due course. Having captured both the British Amateur and Open titles in one season, Barrington pushed his horizons further afield and took most of the world's major titles. Only one main amateur title eluded him, the World Championship, which must have been a bitter disappointment for the man who conquered through sheer effort and a steel mind.

Barrington's number of Open triumphs now stands second only to Hashim Khan's, but his reign has never been without threat, and indeed, defeat.

Other British players vying for places in the hall of fame include Michael Oddy and Nigel Broomfield, amateurs at their peaks in the late fifties and early sixties. Neither quite broke through, although Oddy reached the final of the Open only to lose to Taleb.

Oddy's successor as British amateur champion was Ken Hiscoe of Australia in 1962, the first Australian to write his name into the international record books. Although Hiscoe has not won the Open title his presence in Australian squash has probably been as great as his colleague Geoff Hunt.

Hiscoe, from Sydney, learnt a valuable piece of advice from Dardir with reference to the importance of the volley. Dardir extolled the precept that 'squash has only three walls. If there is no back wall you'll have to volley and the tactical advantage gained is enormous.' Hiscoe's principles of attack, even blatant aggression, honed from superb stroke-play, embodied the essence of the Australian dominance that was really to come to power in 1967 with the first World Amateur Championships.

Australia won the team event and Hunt the individual title. This result was to be repeated three times to extend the reign over six years. A further two years of life were added by virtue of the World Amateur Championships being held in South Africa in 1973, when once again Australia triumphed – this time Cam Nancarrow took the individual title – in the absence of the Pakistan team, which must have been favoured to break the Australians' grip.

The leading exponent from Australia during this period was Geoff Hunt, twice Open Champion, whose power play and phenomenal results have occasioned some to liken him to Hashim Khan, even to declare that he is the best ever. The 1975 Open season results in Britain tend to discredit the claims as extravagant, but as Hunt has years ahead of him should he choose to continue playing, predictions are not only dangerous, but simply futile.

On much firmer ground is an examination of the women's game, where two ladies have stood out from the rest so much that no argument can be proffered from any corner.

Janet Shardlow (nee Morgan) ruled the women's scene from 1949 until 1958 with superior training, mental application, and weight of shot. When she retired no one thought her feat would be equalled let alone beaten, yet three years later a young girl from Australia, Heather Blundell, won the Women's Championship after playing the game for only two years. Nothing and nobody has looked like stopping Mrs Heather McKay, as she now is, since. Heather has rarely dropped a game in the last 14 years, and recently she has been winning the final of the Women's Championship for a loss of a handful of points in about 20 minutes.

The fitness, stamina and ability of Mrs McKay, also a hockey international, make her one of the automatic choices in the all-time greats. Heather and Hashim . . . what a frightening mixed doubles combination!

PLAYER RANKINGS

WORLD
(As approved by the International Squash Professionals Association)

GOGI ALAUDDIN (Pakistan)

1 Qamar Zaman (Pakistan)
2 Geoff Hunt (Australia)
3 Gogi Alauddin (Pakistan)
4 Hiddy Jahan (Pakistan)
5 Mohibullah Khan (Pakistan)
6 Ken Hiscoe (Australia)
7 Jonah Barrington (GB)
8 Cam Nancarrow (Australia)
9 Ahmed Safwat (Egypt)
10 Torsam Khan (Pakistan)
11 Roland Watson (South Africa)
12 Sajjad Muneer (Pakistan)
13 Rehmat Khan (Pakistan)
14 Billy Reedman (Australia)
15 Mohammed Yasin (Pakistan)
16 John Easter (GB)

MEN

Australia (amateur)
1 Mike Donnelly
2 Dave Wright
3 Lionel Robberds
4 Dick Carter
5 Leo Keppell
6 Ray Lewis

Australia (professional)
1 Geoff Hunt
2 Ken Hiscoe
3 Cam Nancarrow
4 Billy Reedman
5 Doug Stephensen

Belgium
1 Peter Masterson
2 Chris Laker
3 Derek Gaw
4 Eric Sheridan
5 Chris Validrey

Denmark
1 Peter Gerlow
2 John Philips
3 Bjarne Poulsen
4 Hans Henrik Haume
5 Fleming Bulow

Finland
1 Roger Jones
2 Kale Lsekinen
3 Harri Bucht
4 Harri Salo
5 Henri Bucht

France (all players)
1 Jeremy Payne
2 Peter Salinson
3 Peter Cogan

France (national)
1 Pierre Barthes
2 Deni Grozdanovitch
3 Jacques Strauss
4 Jean Grandchamp
5 Remy Salmon

Great Britain
1 Philip Ayton
2 Mike Corby
3 John Richardson
4 Peter Verow
5 Stuart Courtney
6 Jonathan Leslie
7 Ian Robinson
8 Ian Nuttall
9 Pat Kirton
10 Paul Millman
11 Kim Bruce-Lockhart
12 Warwick Sabey

Holland
1 Robert Anjema
2 Willem van Rooijen
3 Peter Fangman
4 Rolf Krayenhoff
5 Henk Herok

Germany
1 Ronny Rothenberger
2 Peter Marquardt
3 Joachim Weber
4 Robert Fuestel
5 Klaus von Mallinckrodt

Ireland
1 John McGrath
2 Robert Weir
3 Ben Cranwell
4 Gerry Doherty
5 Bernard O'Gorman

New Zealand
1 N. Barbour
2 T. Johnston
3 H. Broun
4 L. Greene
5 S. O'Dwyer
6 T. Colyer
7 B. Brownlee
8 D. Cotter
9 R. Purser
10 A. Naughton

Pakistan
1 Qamar Zaman
2 Gogi Alauddin
3 Mohibullah Khan
4 Torsam Khan
5 Sajjad Muneer
6 Rehmat Khan
7 Mohammed Yasin
8 Mohammed Saleem
9 Maqsood Ahmed
10 Abdul Rahman

Scotland
1 Kim Bruce-Lockhart
2 Neil Martin
3 Chris Wilson
4 Neil Stewart
5 Alan Minty

MOHAMMED SALEEM (Pakistan)

Sweden
1 Mikael Helstrom
2 Tarras Tovar
3 Frederick af Ekenstam
4 Lars Kvant
5 Leif Leiner

South Africa
1 Roland Watson
2 Dawie Botha
3 Steve Sherren
4 Selwyn Machet
5 Doug Barrow
6 Keith Coppin
7 Dave Scott
8 Alan Colburn
9 Graham Macdonald
10 Philip Timperley

Ulster
1 John McGrath
2 Gerry Doherty
3 David Gotto
4 John Young
5 Cecil Pedlow
6 Gordon Bell
7 Frank McKeever
8 Robin McDonough
9 Harry Bunting
10 Tony Graham

Wales
1 David Jude
2 Robert Dolman
3 James Beattie
4 Ian Carlisle
5 Peter Wilson

Below left: *SELWYN MACHET (South Africa)*

Right: *PETER VEROW (Great Britain)*

WOMEN

Australia
1 Marion Jackman
2 Jenny Irving
3 Sue Newman
4 Lyle Hubinger
5 Margaret Zachariah
6 Chris van Nierop

Great Britain and Ireland
1 Sue Cogswell
2 Jean Wilson
3 Teresa Lawes
4 Jane Courtney
5 Irene Hewitt
6 Fran Marshall
7 Theo Veltman
8 Geraldine Barniville
9 Claire Chapman
10 Karen Gardner

New Zealand
1 J. Webster
2 P. Buckingham
3 C. Fleming
4 J. Lamb
5 R. Davis
6 K. Glenny
7 A. Reilly
8 K. Graham
9 J. Roberts
10 V. McCausland

South Africa
1 Kathy Hardy
2 Jill Eckstein
3 Gay Erskine
4 Irene Hewitt
5 Val Bridgens
6 Di Allan
7 Jill Donaldson
8 Denise Holton
9 Beryl Boon
10 Ann Papenfus

Ulster
1 Dorothy Armstrong
2 Julie Morrison
3 Brenda Quinlan
4 Jennifer Givan
5 Jill Minford
6 Maureen Moore
7 Nuala McMordie
8 Joan Martin
9 Rosemary McKeever
10 Terry Wells

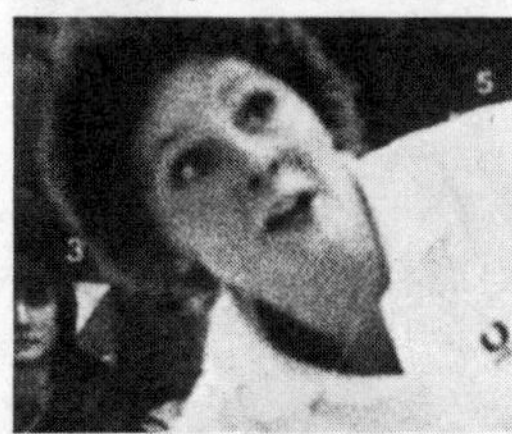

THEO VELTMAN (Great Britain)

CHRIS VAN NIEROP (Australia)

COMMERCIAL SQUASH – ITS BEGINNINGS, FORM, AND FUTURE

Rex Guppy

Ten years ago, only a handful of squash clubs owned by individuals existed. Today over 100 clubs are commercially operated.

What sparked this apparent boom was nothing unique in Britain's business world – simply a combination of frustration and foresight. The frustration was felt by a few keen players of modest class who were unable to play the game they enjoyed through lack of court space; so they had to build courts on which to play. The foresight was a vision of the unique merits and qualities that squash has over every other sport: it is a game for the many, not the few.

In the early 1960s, during the days of Britain's stop-go economy, credit squeezes, and a bank-rate of five per cent, a few entrepreneurs put their ideas to the test. Some viewed their efforts and enthusiasm with a mixture of alarm and amazement, but curiosity was roused as to the type of budget on which these operations could be viable. This had to be calculated remembering that squash was traditionally played at school, university, in the armed forces, and only during the winter months.

Therefore, the first commercial clubs were designed and built entirely on the back of other businesses. Freddy Cockerill of ABC Cinemas, for example, carried the responsibility for their first club built on the car park adjacent to a cinema. Joe Telford and Roy Perkins, a builder and a solicitor respectively, together established Northwood. This was the way in which clubs were developed in the mid- and late 1960s.

From the establishment centres of squash there were fears about the impact of commercialism. Would the newcomers take over the game they had nurtured? The extra court space was welcome, but the high subscriptions and court fees appeared unfair. Up until that stage squash had been virtually free. For county and leading players this is still the case.

But like every new venture, appearances can be misleading and so it proved in commercial squash. From the outside it all looked easy. Build a few courts, add changing-rooms and a bar, and watch the car park fill up. Well, during peak hours the car park is full – but only with one person to each vehicle! The design and building of a squash court also looked deceptively simple. Nothing but a box. Why then should one court cost more than a complete house? But it does. The club full of people? Yes, at peak times; but during the day and on Saturdays, clubs can be like morgues – and squash players, as a general rule, are not social drinkers.

Staffing is not easy. Owners and managers put in over 90 hours a week regularly, and there are not many businesses that are open 15 hours a day, seven days a week, 52 weeks a year. On overheads, apart from the accepted items of rates, gas, water, and electricity, the biggest bill is maintenance. To keep a club in top condition is a *full-time* job and an expensive commitment.

As I said earlier, the first of the few had little or nothing on which to base their financial budgets. All they could follow were the subscriptions being charged by 'members' clubs' operations – and these were often as low as £3 a year and a shilling an hour for the lights. The first commercial clubs, therefore, made the error of playing the 'numbers game' – hoping that turnover alone would solve the problems of servicing any loans and paying dividends, as well as leaving a surplus for reinvestment.

Unfortunately their example was copied by those who followed, and each club, in unhappy isolation, began a period of financial insecurity. The profits were not there, and yet it was difficult to see how the price for courts could be increased when members' clubs could offer something far cheaper. The answer was to spend more money and build more courts, but without an increase in staff. This policy appeared to work in the late 1960s. Memberships soared . . . and so did inflation. The bank-rate doubled, while building and land costs trebled.

Nevertheless, squash had arrived and everyone felt the benefits. The game was opened up to the public at large. New courts were built and designed for 12 months play, and the uninitiated took to summer squash in vast numbers.

The spin-offs of the commercial clubs' interest in squash are now acknowledged without question. First, the finances of the members' clubs were brought into healthy surplus. Second, member-owned clubs in other spheres, such as rugby, tennis, and golf, saw, in the building of squash courts, a means of solving the financial problems of their less viable sports. Local authorities regarded squash as a means of bringing pleasure to many people while at the same time producing a cash flow. Finally, the commercial clubs opened up the game for the professionals in the fields of coaching, exhibition work, and sponsored tournaments.

As yet, there are no accurate figures on the number of courts or players in the game. The Squash Rackets Association, the game's governing body, have had to adjust to the changes and have not found it easy. Their prime responsibility is to control and regulate the competitive scene and to assist in co-ordinating the various interested parties. These now include the professionals' association, players' association, and international associations.

Until 1973, all commercial clubs operated in a vacuum. There was no central means of aid and with the introduction of value added tax, higher rating assessments, and corporation tax, these clubs faced the competition with concern. The members' clubs, for example, were making good profits by the early 1970s, while only charging half the fees of the nearest commercial concern. Such a situation was hardly surprising, for they pay neither VAT nor corporation tax, and can attract low-interest sports council grant aid.

Neither do local authority sports centres charge subscriptions. They have low court fees, and operate with a rate subsidy. Parallel with member clubs and sports centres, company-owned clubs emerged with subsidised sports facilities for their staff.

This is the type of competition that is slowing the growth of commercial clubs, quite apart from the effect of land and building costs. To build a six-court club today of modest standard, the basic bill would be £125,000. Such a project would require a subscription within the region of £25 to £30 and a court fee of 60p per half hour per player. Such figures, though apparently high, must be charged if commercial clubs are to continue operating on a viable basis.

How then do I view the future? First, I think competition is good; good for the game, for the players, and for the clubs. The commercial operators must face up to the price struggle in a realistic way. They must charge a viable rate, but give a service meriting such prices, i.e. facilities must be of a higher standard to justify the extra cost. This applies to courts, changing rooms, and club rooms, as well as general club efficiency.

Through the newly-formed proprietors' federation (BSRPF), combined skills and expertise on the running and advancement of commercial clubs can be brought to a high level and so encourage further building.

At present, the big growth area for British squash lies in council-operated sports centres. This is where the Sports Council and rate money is being applied. But having said that, I still believe there will be those who, despite the difficulties, will pursue their object of building a club to support the game they enjoy.

Rex Guppy is proprietor of Kingswood Squash Club, Basildon, Essex, and chairman of the British Squash Rackets Proprietors Federation.

THE ROLE OF THE SRA

Peter Woods

The SRA has played a unique role in the development of squash. It was the first national association to be formed, and as individual playing members made contacts throughout other countries overseas, so its influence and guidance helped other national associations to develop.

As squash's popularity has grown in recent years, in countries where perhaps only one small club exists, enthusiasts have increasingly sought the expertise and experience of the SRA in promoting the game. Indeed, the International and European Squash Rackets Federations came into being (in 1967 and 1973 respectively) largely through the work of SRA officials and players.

RECENT DEVELOPMENTS

The characteristics of the game are the prime reason for its growth. But without the initiative that many individuals have shown in promoting it, little of that growth would have occurred. The realisation of financial viability and the inspiration given to individual players by Jonah Barrington have been the two main catalysts. The image of squash as a sport for 'toffs', like Colonel Blimp, dies hard; but the facts of its spread through all the socio-economic groupings have been set out in the publication *The Case for Squash*, and are well appreciated by those who are in touch with sports and social clubs, schools, universities, and municipal centres throughout the country. The game already has more participants than lawn tennis, and with some justification the numbers are expected to top the million by 1981.

As recently as 1967, the first major effort was made to utilise the game's financial potential. Since then the proportion of members' clubs, operated commercially, has reached some 35 per cent and the number of courts considered as the minimum for a unit has grown from four to eight.

Many technical changes in materials and design (e.g. Banbury and Bicester Courts, and lighting) have been seen as ways and means of reducing construction and maintenance costs. The most significant change has been the development of the full glass back wall, only five years ago. Not only does this innovation enable more people to watch, but it gives an opportunity for the game to be brought to a much wider public via television. The implications of this publicity for the Association, and for clubs, sponsors, and professional players, are only just beginning to be realised.

CENTRAL ADMINISTRATION

Clearly stated in the objects of the Association is that it is 'the central authority . . . in all matters connected with the organisation and playing of the game . . . and in the interests of amateurs and professionals alike', indicating that means for influence and control had to be established.

In exerting its authority, the SRA must rely upon the full cooperation, goodwill, and support of affiliated clubs, individual members, and hundreds of voluntary organisers, to be fully effective. The key element in the structure is the county association, through which most of the practical work with clubs and players is done; and it will remain the key, no matter what reorganisation may be introduced. However, the span of control for the SRA at the centre would be impossible if there were no intermediate level between county and SRA. Counties are therefore grouped into areas.

Originally, six areas were formed for competition administration and coaching purposes; but the growth of the game in many counties made it necessary to spread the workload. So there are now nine areas in operation under the auspices of the SRA headquarters in London.

Between 1945 and 1967, the Association was headed by an executive which formed policy and conducted general business. It was assisted by a finance and general committee, and some sub-committees. But the volume and pressure of work created by the growth of the game forced a change, so that a council with much wider representation from the country became the policy-maker. The conduct of day-to-day affairs was given to a management committee, elected by the council. Sub-committees were used as before.

In 1974 the area representatives were brought on to the management committee so that views held throughout the country could be aired, and have some obvious influence on decision-making.

FINANCE

The total revenue required for the administration of the Association's business is not solely dependent upon the subscriptions of individual members and affiliation fees. These two sources combined have previously represented some 30 per cent of the income, but since 1973 (with the major increase in affiliation fees) the proportion has been closer to 40 per cent. Grant Aid allocated by the Sports Council amounts to a further 30 per cent, while additional revenue may be provided through donations, contributions from industry, and sponsorship.

PROMOTION AND DEVELOPMENT

The Association must have knowledge of both existing and proposed squash facilities so that appropriate guidance may be given to those wishing to provide them, and to those wishing to play. The number of enquiries and proposals put to the staff is increasing annually. It is a task of major importance to bring the game into places of education at all levels, and to make it available to all levels of society and income. The decentralisation to areas of much of the practical work involved, including general and technical advice on projects, is essential so that local knowledge can be fully exploited.

The promotion of the game is stimulated by the public relations activities of not only the SRA (both members and players), but also via national and provincial media. This involves the development of better communications within the Association to provide knowledge of what is going on, and to give a better understanding of the problems involved and the reasons for decisions at all levels. It also involves the production of material, instructional and informative, for internal and external use.

ORGANISATION AND PLAYING

The tournament sub-committee, together with those for referees and markers, and selection and seeding, are responsible for establishing the pattern and conduct of events; their work is frequently through area, county, and local tournament organisers where the closest communication with the appropriate voluntary organisers and officials is essential. The fixture list and its successful operation requires initially the examination of international events, promotions, sponsorships, and requests from clubs for events: and then the sorting out of the consequent major jigsaw puzzle.

The policy of the SRA in respect of sponsorship, promotions and the negotiations with the newly-formed International Squash Players' Association and the Squash Rackets Professionals' Association is recommended to the management committee by the tournament sub-committee and then implemented by it.

The selection of representative sides and individuals, whether at national level or for the SRA for play in championships, international matches, and tours overseas, comes from advice on local players and during the competitive season is regularly converted into the list of top 20 players by the selectors.

SETTING AND MAINTENANCE OF STANDARDS

The setting of the rules of the game is established by the

ISRF but any proposed changes in rule or interpretation is examined within the Association; the conduct of play regulated by the standard of officiating is of the greatest significance to the future of the game. The effects of the rules and their interpretation are closely watched, and guidance is given when requested.

The Association is closely concerned in the standard of the ball used, the specifications of the racket, and the court, including dimensions and materials used. Examination and testing of new materials and equipment is becoming a more frequent occurrence as the game's growth encourages firms in the leisure industry to move into squash.

PROVISION OF SERVICES

The Association has been constantly developing and broadening all the services offered; the most significant is the coaching service, which through the implementation of a five-year plan (1972) is bringing coaching to clubs, schools, and sports centres at all levels; the decentralisation of much of this work through area coaching representatives and counties is being extended. The service includes the production and provision of films, publications, posters, slides, and instructional notes.

The Association's advisory service includes all aspects of planning, construction, and running of facilities as well as the setting up and operation of tournaments, leagues, and exhibitions. Advice on maintenance and repair to all squash facilities (free to affiliated members) is comprehensive and of great significance when so much construction is being completed each year; some unfortunately not to the recommended specifications. This work also is gradually being decentralised to areas.

STRENGTH AND VIABILITY OF THE ASSOCIATION

The status of the Association is very high internationally and must be retained. Its image at home has in times of major change suffered inevitable setbacks, but those who are working for the game through the SRA will establish a national respect and standing of the highest order.

The financial viability of the Association depends upon the success it has in finding revenue to provide for the services considered essential to the fulfilment of its objects, and in limiting expenditure to the work of appropriate priority. Above all the continued loyalty of its members, individual and affiliated, is the keynote to its strength and the successsful achievement of its work,

Peter Woods is secretary of the Squash Rackets Association.

CHAMPIONSHIP ROLLS

Throughout this section the season 1972–73 is indicated by the date '1972' and similarly for all seasons.

THE OPEN CHAMPIONSHIP

1930 Championship instituted. C. R. Read (Queen's Club) designated champion.

*1930 D. G. Butcher (Conservative) bt C. R. Read (Queen's), 9-6, 9-5, 9-5 at Queen's, and 9-3, 9-5, 9-3 at Conservative Club.

1931 D. G. Butcher (Conservative) bt C. Arnold (Bath), 9-0, 9-0, 9-0 at Conservative, and 9-3, 9-0, 9-5 at Bath Club.

*1932 F. D. Amr Bey bt D. G. Butcher (Conservative), 9-0, 9-7, 9-1 at Conservative, and 5-9, 6-9, 9-2, 9-1, 9-0 at Bath Club.

*1934 F. D. Amr Bey bt D. G. Butcher (Conservative), 9-4, 8-10, 10-8, 9-0 at Conservative, and 9-6, 6-9, 9-2, 0-9, 9-5 at Bath Club.

*1935 F. D. Amr Bey bt J. Dear (Prince's), 9-3, 6-9, 8-10, 9-2, 9-4 at Bath Club, and 9-4, 9-7, 3-9, 9-7 at RAC.

*1936 F. D. Amr Bey bt J. Dear (Prince's), 9-7, 7-9, 9-7, 5-9, 9-6 at RAC, and 9-7, 8-10, 9-1, 9-6 at Bath Club.

*1937 F. D. Amr Bey bt J. Dear (Prince's), 10-8, 10-8, 4-9, 1-9, 9-4 at RAC, and 9-7, 8-10, 9-6, 9-5 at Bath Club.

*1938 P. Dear (Prince's) bt A. E. Biddle (Junior Carlton), 5-9, 9-6, 5-9, 9-6, 9-5 and 6-9, 9-1, 9-2, 9-6.

*1946 M. A. Karim (Gezira SC) bt J. Dear (Queen's), 9-4, 9-1, 9-3 at Lansdowne Club, and 5-9, 7-9, 9-8, 9-7, 9-4 at RAC.

1947 M. A. Karim (Gezira SC) bt J. Dear (Queen's), 9-5, 9-3, 5-9, 1-9, 10-8 at Lansdowne Club.

1948 M. A. Karim (Gesira SC) bt B. C. Phillips, 9-4, 9-2, 9-10, 9-4 at Lansdowne Club.

1949 M. A. Karim (Gezira SC) bt A. Bari (Cricket Club of India, Bombay), 9-4, 9-2, 9-7 at Lansdowne Club.

1950 Hashim Khan (RPAF Peshawar) bt M. A. Karim (Gezira SC) 9-5, 9-0, 9-0 at Lansdowne Club.

1951 Hashim Khan (RPAF Peshawar) bt M. A. Karim (Gezira SC), 9-5, 9-7, 9-0 at Lansdowne Club.

1952 Hashim Khan (RPAF Risalpur) bt R. B. R. Wilson, 9-2, 8-10, 9-1, 9-0 at Lansdowne Club.

Torsam Khan's fiercely competitive spirit got him into trouble on several occasions in 1975 but no one can deny the will to win shown by the rising young Pakistani star.

1953 Hashim Khan (RPAF Risalpur) bt Azam Khan (RPAF Peshawar), 6-9, 9-6, 9-6, 7-9, 9-5 at Lansdowne Club.
1954 Hashim Khan (RPAF Risalpur) bt Azam Khan (RPAF Peshawar), 9-7, 7-9, 9-7, 5-9, 9-7 at Lansdowne Club.
1955 Hashim Khan (RPAF Risalpur) bt Roshan Khan (RPN Karachi), 9-4, 9-2, 5-9, 9-5 at Lansdowne Club.
1956 Roshan Khan (RPN Karachi) bt Hashim Khan (RPAF Risalpur), 6-9, 9-5, 9-2, 9-1 at Lansdowne Club.
1957 Hashim Khan (Pakistan Air Force) bt Azam Khan (New Grampians SRC), 9-7, 6-9, 9-6, 9-7 at Lansdowne Club.
1958 Azam Khan (New Grampians SRC) bt Mohibullah Khan (Pakistan Air Force), 9-5, 9-0, 9-1 at RAC.
1959 Azam Khan (New Grampians SRC) bt Roshan Khan (Pakistan Navy), 9-1, 9-0, 9-0 at RAC.
1960 Azam Khan (New Grampians SRC) bt Mohibullah Khan (Pakistan Air Force), 6-9, 9-1, 9-4, 0-9, 9-2 at RAC.
1961 Azam Khan (New Grampians SRC) bt Mohibullah Khan (Pakistan Air Force), 9-6, 7-9, 10-8, 2-9, 9-4 at RAC.
1962 Mohibullah Khan (Pakistan) bt A. F. A. Taleb (UAR), 9-4, 5-9, 3-9, 10-8, 9-6 at the Lansdowne and Royal Aero Clubs.
1963 A. F. A. Taleb (UAR) bt M. A. Oddy (Scotland), 9-3, 9-7, 9-0, at the Lansdowne and Royal Aero Clubs.
1964 A. F. A. Taleb (UAR) bt I. Amin (UAR) 9-0, 0-9, 9-1, 9-6 at the Lansdowne and Royal Aero Clubs.
1965 A. F. A. Taleb (UAR) bt A. Jawaid (Pakistan), 9-6, 5-9, 9-3, 9-1 at the Lansdowne and Royal Aero Clubs.
1966 J. P. Barrington (Ireland) bt A. Jawaid (Pakistan), 9-2, 6-9, 9-2, 9-2 at the Lansdowne and Royal Aero Clubs.
1967 J. P. Barrington (Ireland) bt A. F. A. Taleb (UAR), 9-6, 9-0, 9-5 at the Lansdowne and Royal Aero Clubs.
1968 G. B. Hunt (Australia) bt C. Nancarrow (Australia), 9-5, 9-4, 9-0 at Edgbaston Priory Club.
1969 J. P. Barrington (Ireland) bt G. B. Hunt (Australia), 9-7, 3-9, 3-9, 9-4, 9-4 at Abbeydale Park SRC.
1970 J. P. Barrington (Ireland) bt A. Jawaid (Pakistan), 9-1, 9-2, 9-6 at Abbeydale Park SRC.
1971 J. P. Barrington (Ireland) bt G. B. Hunt (Australia), 0-9, 9-7, 10-8, 6-9, 9-7 at Abbeydale Park SRC.
1972 J. P. Barrington (Ireland) bt G. Alauddin (Pakistan), 9-4, 9-3, 9-2.
1973 G. B. Hunt (Australia) w.o. M. Yasin (Pakistan), injured, scratched at Abbeydale Park SRC.
1974 Q. Zaman (Pakistan) bt G. Alauddin (Pakistan) 9-7, 9-6, 9-1, at Wembley.

**From its institution until 1947 the championship was played on the challenge system, with home and away matches and the stipulation that a third match should be played if the results of the first two were level.*

THE AMATEUR CHAMPIONSHIP

Played in 1922 at Lord's, from 1923 to 1938 at the Bath Club. from 1946 to 1957, and 1962 to 1970 at the Lansdowne Club, and from 1958 to 1961 at the Royal Automobile Club.

1922 T. O. Jameson bt J. E. Palmer-Tomkinson, 17-15, 12-15, 15-0
1923 T. O. Jameson bt C. le C. Browning, 15-11, 16-14
1924 W. D. Macpherson bt J. E. Palmer-Tomkinson, 17-14, 8-15, 15-7
1925 V. A. Cazalet bt J. E. Palmer-Tomkinson, 15-8, 12-15, 18-17
1926 J. E. Palmer-Tomkinson bt V. A. Cazalet, 9-5, 9-7, 7-9, 9-6
1927 V. A. Cazalet bt H. W. Backhouse, 4-9, 9-6, 3-9, 10-8, 9-4
1928 W. D. Macpherson bt V. A. Cazalet, 9-3, 9-1, 5-9, 1-9, 9-1
1929 V. A. Cazalet bt W. F. Basset, 9-2, 9-5, 9-7
1930 V. A. Cazalet bt K. C. Gandar-Dower, 9-2, 6-9, 7-9,9-6, 9-2
1931 F. D. Amr Bey bt W. D. Macpherson, 9-7, 9-6, 4-9, 5-9, 9-0
1932 F. D. Amr Bey bt E. Snell, 9-1, 9-0, 9-4
1933 F. D. Amr Bay bt G. O. M. Jameson, 9-0, 9-2, 9-4
1934 C. P. Hamilton bt D. M. Backhouse, 9-7, 9-0, 9-4
1935 F. D. Amr Bey bt E. Snell, 9-1, 9-0, 9-1
1936 F. D. Amr Bey bt E. Snell, 9-4, 9-0, 9-2
1937 F. D. Amr Bey bt J. F. Stokes, 9-3, 9-4, 9-2
1938 K. C. Gandar-Dower bt D. I. Burnett, 2-9, 10-8, 9-6, 10-8
1939 to 1945 No competition
1946 N. F. Borrett bt J. A. Gillies, 9-3, 9-6, 9-3
1947 N. F. Borrett bt J. R. Thompson, 9-2, 9-4, 9-4
1948 N. F. Borrett bt B. C. Phillips, 9-2, 9-4, 9-2
1949 N. F. Borrett bt H. J. A. Dagnall, 9-4, 9-5, 10-8
1950 N. F. Borrett bt G. Hildick-Smith (South Africa), 9-6, 10-8, 9-1
1951 G. Hildick-Smith (South Africa) bt B. C. Phillips, 9-3, 9-2, 9-2
1952 A. Fairbairn bt R. B. R. Wilson, 9-2, 9-2, 4-9, 9-1
1953 A. Fairbairn bt R. B. R. Wilson, 7-9, 9-1, 9-6, 9-7
1954 R. B. R. Wilson bt A. Fairbairn, 9-7, 8-10, 9-6, 9-4
1955 I. Amin (Egypt) bt R. B. R. Wilson, 4-9, 9-7, 2-9, 9-7, 10-8
1956 R. B. R. Wilson bt D. Callaghan (South Africa) 7-9, 8-10, 9-1, 9-4, 9-6
1957 N. H. R. A. Broomfield bt I. Amin (Egypt), 9-1, 9-7, 9-4
1958 N. H. R. A. Broomfield bt I. Amin (Egypt), 9-2, 9-6, 1-9, 9-7
1959 I. Amin (Egypt) bt T. Shafik (Egypt), 9-7, 0-9, 9-6, 9-5
1960 M. A. Oddy bt I. Amin (Egypt), 9-2, 7-9, 10-8, 9-4
1961 M. A. Oddy bt I. Amin (UAR), 9-5, 3-9, 10-8, 9-1
1962 K. Hiscoe (Australia) bt T. Shafik (UAR), 9-3, 9-7, 5-9, 9-7

1963 A. A. Jawaid (Pakistan) bt T. Shafik (UAR) 7-9, 9-2, 5-9, 9-4, 9-5
1964 A. A. Jawaid (Pakistan) bt G. B. Hunt (Australia), 9-5, 8-10, 9-3, 10-9
1965 A. A. Jawaid (Pakistan) bt R. Carter (Australia), 7-9, 9-2, 9-2, 9-10, 9-6
1966 J. P. Barrington bt R. Carter (Australia), 1-9, 9-6, 7-9, 9-7, 9-6
1967 J. P. Barrington bt M. W. Corby, 9-3, 9-6, 2-9, 9-5
1968 J. P. Barrington bt M. W. Corby, 3-9, 9-1, 9-2, 9-3
1969 G. B. Hunt (Australia) bt A. Jawaid (Pakistan), 9-7, 9-2, 9-0
1970 G. Alauddin (Pakistan) bt W. Reedman (Australia), 9-3, 9-0, 9-5
1971 G. Alauddin (Pakistan) bt M. Asran (Egypt), 6-9, 9-3, 7-9, 9-6, 9-2, at the Lambton Squash Club.
1972 C. Nancarrow (Australia) bt W. Reedman (Australia), 0-9, 9-2, 9-1, 9-7, at the Lambton and New Croydon Squash Clubs.
1973 Mohibullah Khan (Pakistan) bt Qamar Zaman (Pakistan), 9-5, 10-8, 6-9, 7-9, 10-8, at the Lambton and New Croydon Squash Clubs.
1974 Mohibullah Khan (Pakistan) bt Qamar Zaman (Pakistan) 10-8, 9-5, 5-9, 9-5, at Wembley.

WOMEN'S OPEN CHAMPIONSHIP

1921 Miss J. Cave
1922 Miss S. Huntsman
1923 Miss N. Cave
1924 Miss J. Cave
1925 Miss C. Fenwick
1926 Miss C. Fenwick
1927 Miss J. Cave
1928 Miss N. Cave
1929 Miss N. Cave
1930 Miss C. Fenwick
1931 Miss S. Noel
1932 Miss S. Noel
1933 Miss S. Noel
1934 Miss M. E. Lumb
1935 Miss M. E. Lumb
1936 Miss M. E. Lumb
1937 Miss M. E. Lumb
1938 Miss M. E. Lumb
1946 Miss P. J. Curry
1947 Miss P. J. Curry
1948 Miss P. J. Curry
1949 Miss J. R. M. Morgan
1950 Miss J. R. M. Morgan
1951 Miss J. R. M. Morgan
1952 Miss J. R. M. Morgan
1953 Miss J. R. M. Morgan
1954 Miss J. R. M. Morgan
1955 Miss J. R. M. Morgan
1956 Miss J. R. M. Morgan
1957 Miss J. R. M. Morgan
1958 Miss J. R. M. Morgan
1959 Mrs H. Macintosh
1960 Mrs F. Marshall
1961 Miss H. Blundell (Australia)
1962 Miss H. Blundell (Australia)
1963 Miss H. Blundell (Australia)
1964 Miss H. Blundell (Australia)
1965 Mrs H. McKay (Australia)
1966 Mrs H. McKay (Australia)
1967 Mrs H. McKay (Australia)
1968 Mrs H. McKay (Australia)
1969 Mrs H. McKay (Australia)
1970 Mrs H. McKay (Australia)
1971 Mrs H. McKay (Australia)
1972 Mrs H. McKay (Australia)
1973 Mrs H. McKay (Australia)
1974 Mrs H. McKay (Australia)